RUSSIAN
CIVIL-MILITARY
RELATIONS:
Putin's Legacy

Also by Thomas Gomart:

Russie.Nei.Visions 2008, Understanding Russia and the New Independent States, (ed. with Tatiana Kastouéva-Jean), Paris, Ifri, 2008.

Russie.Nei.Visions 2007, Understanding Russia and the New Independent States, (ed. with Tatiana Kastouéva-Jean), Paris, Ifri, 2007.

Russie.Nei.Visions 2006, Understanding Russia and the New Independent States, (ed. with Tatiana Kastouéva-Jean), Paris, Ifri, 2006.

Double détente : Les relations franco-soviétiques de 1958 à 1964 [Double detente: Franco-Soviet relations 1958–1964], Paris, Publications de la Sorbonne, 2003, preface by Robert Frank. (Jean-Baptiste Duroselle award—Institut de France).

Les Rapports russo-français vus de Moscou [French–Russian relations: A view from Moscow], Paris, Ifri, 2002, foreword by Dominique David.

RUSSIAN
CIVIL-MILITARY
RELATIONS:
Putin's Legacy

Thomas Gomart

CARNEGIE ENDOWMENT
FOR INTERNATIONAL PEACE
WASHINGTON DC ▪ MOSCOW ▪ BEIJING ▪ BEIRUT ▪ BRUSSELS

ifri

Carnegie Endowment for International Peace
1779 Massachusetts Avenue, N.W., Washington, D.C. 20036
202-483-7600, Fax 202-483-1840
www.CarnegieEndowment.org

The Carnegie Endowment for International Peace normally does not take institutional positions on public policy issues; the views and recommendations presented in this publication do not necessarily represent the views of the Carnegie Endowment, its officers, staff, or trustees.

To order, contact:
Hopkins Fulfillment Service
P.O. Box 50370, Baltimore, MD 21211-4370
1-800-537-5487 or 1-410-516-6956
Fax 1-410-516-6998

Cover design by Sese-Paul Design
Composition by Oakland Street Publishing

Library of Congress Cataloging-in-Publication data
   Gomart, Thomas.
     Russian civil-military relations: Putin's legacy / Thomas Gomart.
       p. cm.
     Includes bibliographical references and index.
     ISBN 978-0-87003-241-7 (pbk.) -- ISBN 978-0-87003-242-4 (cloth) 1.
Civil-military relations--Russia (Federation) 2. Putin, Vladimir Vladimirovich,
1952- I. Title.

   JN6693.5.C58G66 2008
   322'.50947--dc22   2008020087

11 10 09 08 07 06   1 2 3 4 5   1st Printing 2008

Contents

Foreword

The first major public event under Russia's newly inaugurated President Dmitry Medvedev was a military parade in Moscow's Red Square on May 9, 2008. For the first time since the collapse of the Soviet Union, the parade included military hardware, from the SS-25 Topol intercontinental ballistic missiles to the Tu-160 Blackjack strategic bombers. The message to the outside world was clear: Russia is back, also as a military power, with a global nuclear reach. The message to the domestic audience was no less obvious: the armed forces are the ultimate symbol of the state's power, in which every citizen can take pride. *The army and the people are one*, as they used to repeat in Soviet days. Among the ordinary Muscovites, watching the low-altitude flybys of the bombers, fighters, and tankers, some grumbled at the costly extravaganza; many more approved of it.

The Victory Day parade was also Medvedev's first function as commander-in-chief. Minutes after his inauguration two days before, he was presented with the "nuclear briefcase," the modern version of the scepter and orb, and thus became the supreme boss of the million men under arms in Russia. During the eight-year tenure of his predecessor, Vladimir Putin (2000–2008), presidential control over the armed services was strengthened. The military had to accept the reduction of the role of the General Staff in favor of the office of the Minister of Defense. The minister, in turn, is no longer a career officer; of the last two, one was a political operative, and the other one a financial manager.

On the other hand, Putin's presidency was marked by the ascendancy of the representatives of the power sector, i.e., military, police, and especially security services officers, collectively known as *siloviki*, giving the political system the air of a militocracy. Rather than the state and society controlling its guardians and keepers, it was the keepers occupying many important positions in the state and the economy. Putin, however, did not build a national security state. Formal institutions were trumped by the informal networks.

Under Putin, the mission of military reform was declared accomplished. The United States was de facto reinstated as Russia's potential adversary, even as the word *partnership* was reserved for summit declarations. The resumption, for the first time since the end of the Cold War, of high-profile strategic air patrols to the United States, United Kingdom, and Japanese borders overshadowed a rather modest program to modernize the military's rapidly aging arsenals. Conscription was retained, but its term was cut in half to reflect the shortfall in manpower. Hazing continued unabated, but with fewer people complaining as the Russian military lived down to the description of the Red army as a workers-and-peasants force.

These issues, and many more, are researched in depth by Thomas Gomart, a leading French student of Russia and its relations with the West. From his vantage position at the Institut français de relations internationales in Paris, and through his many trips to Russia, Gomart has been able to confront the contemporary theory of civil-military relations and the realities of today's Russia. He rightly focuses on the Putin presidency, which has given the country's institutions their present shape, but he reaches deeper into Russia's post-communist and Soviet history, and subjects the evidence he has amassed to the rich template of Western theory.

It is my pleasure to recommend this book by Thomas Gomart to all those who are interested in the transformation of Russia, which is still an open-ended process, and which remains an important factor not only for Russia's direct neighbors, but to the international system more broadly, including in its strategic component. The Russian army, which for decades had opposed the West, and did not quite become its ally since the end of that confrontation, merits sustained attention. As the old saying goes, it is never as strong as it wants to look, but is never as feeble as it at times appears.

Dmitri Trenin
Moscow
May 2008

Acknowledgments

I am grateful to Dominique David and Etienne de Durand, the first readers and supporters of this essay. Nicola Bigwood kindly translated the first draft. The contribution of my team at IFRI was also a highly valuable one. Sincere thanks are due to Adrian Dellecker, Dominic Fean, Tatiana Kastouéva-Jean, and Catherine Méniane for their consistent help. At the Carnegie Endowment for International Peace, I would like to thank warmly Mark Medish and Lilia Shevtsova for their enthusiasm and support. Special thanks are due to Dmitri Trenin and Martha Brill Olcott. The publication process was as pleasant as it was efficient thanks to Carrie Mullen, Ilonka Oszvald, and editor Marcia Kramer.

Introduction

From abroad, the map of power in Russia is always difficult to read. It is nevertheless essential to do so in order to assess the broader objectives of a country that is in the process of reestablishing itself on the international stage. Today, following Vladimir Putin's two terms as president, Russia appears to be a much more assertive country, one that is quite strong and impressive in macroeconomic terms. Its robust growth stands in stark contrast with the Yeltsin period. At the same time, Russia has regained genuine freedom of action on the international stage: The Russian comeback is one of the most significant transformations in international relations since 2000.

Conceptions of the distribution of power are frequently centered upon the Kremlin and are crisscrossed by closely linked forces. At first glance, Russia's current regime is characterized by neither a separation of powers nor a clear distinction between public policies but, on the contrary, by the merging of responsibilities and confusion over the competing levels of leadership—all concealed behind a hierarchy and a recentralization of power.

To understand Russian governance today, it is essential to understand the roots of its "specificity." Russian specificity can be defined as a particular type of governance inherited from both the czarist and Soviet past and consisting of power concentrated in the leader's hands; political implementation of law; refusal to establish clearly identified counterweights; and the leader's unwillingness to delegate authority. Russia draws a large portion of its specificity from tangled networks: political, judicial, media-related, economic, and security.

Underlying all this are civil-military relations—basically defined as the chain of political and military means and ends implemented by the state at the highest level. These civil-military relations directly affect the decision-making process within the ruling elite, as well as the links between the presidential leadership and the security community, the business community, and finally, society. The relationship also affects the structure of the security community and, consequently, the atmosphere within the elite and society.

As a nuclear superpower, the USSR allocated the majority of its resources to the security community—the armed forces, the security services, and the ministries in charge of security, whose primary purpose was the protection of the state—and granted it a privileged rank in society. This book is based on the assumption that the collapse of the USSR led to a socioeconomic transition that was as far-reaching as it was brutal, but that avoided genuine politico-military transformation, and that much of Russia's specificity can be explained through the disjunction of these two processes. From this point of view, understanding the evolution of civil-military relations in Russia is indispensable to understanding the "Putin system" and how it will define Russia in the years to come.

This book aims to investigate Putin's legacy on civil-military relations in Russia to decipher the impact of the relationship on how power was distributed while Putin served as president, as well as to anticipate changes beyond 2008. Civil-military relations are deeply rooted in Russian strategic culture—they were part of a specific national mind-set in preparing, maintaining, or employing force to achieve political objectives long before Putin came to power. Conversely, even incremental changes in the balance between the civil and military spheres are one of the most efficient ways to alter the strategic culture. Dealing with civil-military relations consequently implies a dual-track approach.

As Putin's handpicked successor, Dmitry Medvedev assumes the presidency of the Russian Federation—with Putin as his prime minister—civil-military relations will be at the core of his leadership due to the deep-rooted tradition of the personalization of power in Russia and the consistently sensitive relationship between the presidency and the security community in charge of protecting the state from both internal and external threats. With this in mind, this book presents a threefold argument by analyzing power as a capacity, both at the individual and institutional levels, to mobilize and direct moral and material resources.

Putin's legacy on civil-military relations is far from insignificant. Compared with Boris Yeltsin, who paid no attention to this issue except in relation to Chechnya, Vladimir Putin was seen by the security community as a professional, a sort of *primus inter pares*. There is no doubt that he succeeded in achieving significant progress, both directly and indirectly. Putin's leadership was characterized by the search for a new institutional balance within the security community and the judicious involvement of the presidential leadership. However, Putin also believed that any attempt to implement a policy should respect Russian political culture. In other words, being pragmatic in his approach to policy and open in his approach to problem solving, Vladimir Putin was very cautious when it came to making changes, especially in the security field.

This leads to the second argument, which is a domestic one. The relationship between the civil and military institutions accurately reflects Putin's power, both in terms of ambitions and limitations, and is key to understanding his leadership because of the great difficulties he encountered while trying to change an idiosyncratic bureaucracy. Implementing reform and changing institutional balances is a slow, painful, and frustrating process everywhere. In Russia, having a clear vision of the relationship between the civil and military spheres helps to illustrate how Putin's policies were implemented by providing insight into the official wish to reform at the top versus the reluctance to reform coming from different parts of the security community. In other words, an analysis of the relationship serves to fuel the debate on the conservatism and authoritarianism that have prevailed in Russian politics under Putin.

The final argument is primarily related to external issues. The elite and large parts of the population consider Russia's great-power status on the international scene as fundamental to their identity. Many years after the collapse of the USSR, Russia continues to promote a foreign policy rationale based largely on the notion of *derzhavnichestvo*—that Russia is either a great power or it is nothing. Civil-military relations are a key element of this view. There is certainly a parallel between the evolution of civil and military relations under Putin and the evolution of Russian foreign policy: Both processes have been, and will continue to be, closely linked.

For many reasons, experts on Russia ignored civilian-military relations during the past few years. That is not to say that nothing was done in this field. The truth, as will be shown, is quite the opposite, but it means that many external observers have preferred to focus on the other characteristics of Putin's power. In comparison, civil and military relations were much more closely scrutinized during the 1990s. This is understandable in light of numerous events and factors: an attempted coup in August 1991 by those nostalgic for the Soviet era; an October 1993 parliamentary revolt led by General Alexander Vladimirovich Rutskoy that was suppressed by tanks; the role of military personnel in political life (advocated openly by General Alexander Lebed and covertly by General Alexander V. Korzhakov, who was more than just Yeltsin's bodyguard); the weakness of Boris Yeltsin's power; and particularly the first Chechnya war (1994–1996).

The development of the balance between civilian and military institutions was therefore presented as one of the determining factors in the transition from the communist system toward a democratic regime, enabling Russian and Western models to converge. The importance accorded to them was reinforced by Russia's former satellites in Europe, for whom the transition was accompanied by a complete overhaul of their own civil-military balance, with the double incentive of emancipation from Moscow and integration into the North Atlantic Treaty Organization (NATO).

Although the subject of civil-military relations did not fully disappear with Vladimir Putin's coming to power in March 2000, there are three main reasons it was not given the same importance in analyses of the Russian regime during his two terms.

First, Putin's wish to "destroy the oligarchs as a class" was a brilliant example of successful political communication. As a highly popular slogan inside Russia, it drew the political class, the business community, the media, the expert community together, along with public opinion. The battle against the oligarchy, combined with the redefinition of center-to-regions relations, was presented by politicians and the media, both within Russia and abroad, as being at the heart of the stabilization process and the reinforcement of presidential authority carried out by Putin and his close associates. Talk of the "vertical of power," the "dictatorship of law," and "managed democracy" saturated the Kremlin's discourse during Putin's regime, and also—indeed even more so—analyses of the regime. No doubt this diverted attention from more perennial traits of the organization of power—traits stemming from the very nature of civil-military relations.

Second, Putin emphasized from the outset the need to reform the military, both for operational and social reasons, taking into account the degradation in the officers' living conditions—not to mention those of conscripts—during the Yeltsin years. Since the fall of the USSR, this reform was the third attempt at overhauling the armed forces, coming after ones initiated by Pavel Grachev in 1992 and Igor Sergeyev in 1997. The latest plan to reform the military, prepared by Sergey Ivanov, was endorsed by the Duma in July 2003. Its implementation was one of the main issues at stake in civil-military relations from 2004 to 2008. The resumption of military operations in the Caucasus in August 1999 and the tacit support of the military were decisive factors in

Putin's incredibly rapid rise to power. His plan to restore Russian power on the international stage involved regaining military credibility vis-à-vis the countries of the Commonwealth of Independent States (CIS) and, to a lesser extent, in relation to other great or regional powers. This plan was strongly supported by the security community, which had been in constant crisis under Yeltsin.

Third, Putin manifested his personal interest in military matters, and security issues more broadly, which shaped his vision of the world as much as they did the organization of his power. To some extent, he considered himself a professional in this business. Incidentally, under Putin, the center of the debate shifted from the nature of civil-military relations, which is mainly a political issue, to the details of military reform, which are a more technical matter. This shift—intended to give the Russian Federation a military tool adapted to its international and regional ambitions—did not happen purely by chance.

In this sense, if discussion of reform remains focused on operational implications, the issue of civil-military relations is outdated, having been severed from the transition process by both the Russian elite and the expert community. This lack of interest explains in part the numerous comments, either incomplete or biased, on Putin's regime, which is mostly presented as a new form of authoritarianism. In the eyes of a good number of commentators, especially in the West, Putin will always be tainted by his original affiliation with the intelligence services. Yet this is not enough to explain his trajectory or his choices.

The numerous analyses focusing on oligarchs, the restriction of civil liberties, and the control of the main opposition forces have resulted not so much in the army and security services' being neglected, but in their being perceived as connected to the consolidation of Putin's power. Yet this process, while indisputably explained in part by Putin's personal leanings, is also the product of the Russian system's structural constraints. The system encourages a highly personalized power structure, in which all the levers of power and enormous resources are at the leader's disposal.

The problem is that this concentration of power induces a confusion of responsibilities below the presidential level. An analysis of how the different levels of responsibility interact and of the outcome of such interactions should enable an assessment of Putin's capacity for decision making or, on the contrary, his tendency to be indecisive and careful.

The aim of this book is neither to absolve Putin and his entourage from responsibility for the legacy of civil-military relations nor to attribute it directly to them. The aim is to highlight the constitutive nature of civil-military relations, despite their difficult definition, within the distribution of power in a country where political and military elites have always been deeply intertwined. Western analysts seem to have been slow to understand that, contrary to its former satellites, Moscow could not completely reconstruct its balance of state-military relations from scratch: Russia had to confront its Soviet heritage. In 2008, it remains vital to consider the civilian-military interface, as it affects the security policy that shapes the domestic and foreign policies of a country still in search of its identity.

This book also aims to go beyond the traditional dualism between the Kremlin and the military usually made in studying civil-military relations by introducing a third element: the security services. Putin's actions have resulted in a balance among these three institutional players. Though often overlooked, another key element—the state of war—comes into play here. Whatever the power in question, the decision to use force is never neutral. Until hostages were taken at a school in Beslan in September 2004, Russian authorities presented their activities in Chechnya as an antiterrorist operation. Doing so exacerbated tensions among the Kremlin, the Ministry of Defense, the Ministry of Internal Affairs, and the security services due to issues such as military and civilian losses, collateral damage, regional instability, and international repugnance.

Since Beslan, the authorities have considered themselves to be at war. In other words, despite the Kremlin's discourse on successful "stabilization" in Chechnya, the second Chechnya war was a powerful event that affected Putin's regime from the beginning. Formulating an accurate assessment of the situation in Chechnya remains difficult. Nevertheless, it is worth remembering that during Putin's tenure, the relationship between the civil and military spheres developed against a background of asymmetric warfare. And it is worth questioning how this conflict galvanized other parts of the North Caucasus, such as Ingushetia, Dagestan, Kabardino–Balkaria, and Karachay–Cherkessia, where the situation has been steadily deteriorating.

Despite the gradual decline of interest, the relationship between civil and military institutions has maintained a central role in Russia and will continue to be of interest in the future. Understanding this relationship is indispensable for any prospective work on Russia in regard to three key spheres: regime "democratization," which involves subjecting generals, officers, and soldiers, as well as members of the security services, to the same regulations as citizens; framing security policy and the implications it will have for neighboring countries and other powers; and, finally, the atmosphere prevailing within the elite and Russian society. That is why the issue of civil-military relations merits continued interest, both to anticipate regime developments and to shape the attitude that should be adopted by the regime's main international partners. As with Putin and now with Medvedev, the Russian leader always faces the dilemma of whether to stabilize the state and consequently the country by defending the interests of the ruling minority or to transform the state to support the nascent civil society.

The resolution of this dilemma clearly depends on the evolution of civil-military relations. This leads to the first main question: What exactly is the current state of the relationship of those two formidable institutions in Russia? Specifically, has Putin's leadership through his two terms of office resulted in a rupture—be it rhetorical or real—in the nature of the relationship? By focusing on Putin, these questions call *a priori* for descriptive assessments of his personal position and, by extension, that of his administration in developments within the security community.

In practical terms, such an examination of the relationship between the civil and military spheres involves an investigation into two main aspects of the decision-making process. The first is functional and concerns the operation of the chain of command, which required fundamental reform at the end of the Yeltsin period. At that time, orders could be given at the presidential level, without any implementation at the operational level.

The second is political and concerns the use of force. Force is the basis of any security activity. In theory, the political authority should be able to fix military targets in accordance with objectives and to modulate their intensity. The use of force also implies the acceptance of its immediate effects: that military force kills people and destroys things. In practice, however, it is extremely difficult to regulate the intensity of force according to the objectives being pursued. These difficulties have been particularly apparent in Chechnya. In addition, it appears that all the institutional actors in Russia remain reluctant to openly accept the consequences of using force.

The connection between presidential authority and civil-military relations is worth a reexamination. Undoubtedly, though often unconsciously, debates on models of civil and military relations influence our understanding of current developments. There is, however, a risk of applying Western analytical models inappropriately to the Russian reality. Nevertheless, such theoretical or historical models are indispensable for measuring the discrepancy between models that are compatible with a democratic regime and the activities of a large number of Russian officials—indeed, the Russian system as a whole.

The second main question underlying this book is to what extent the concentration of power at the presidential level is accompanied by overrepresentation of the military and the security services in the decision-making process. For better or worse, the Putin years were characterized by an alleged "militarization" of the ruling class. The argument concerning the regime's militarization will be discussed at length in chapter 3. The close involvement of the security services in civil-military relations renders the notion of militarization even more complicated within the Russian context.

This question is paradoxical, as it implies that in order to modify the balance of power in his favor, Putin supported the rise to power of the so-called *siloviki*. In Russian, "sila" means "force," and the term *siloviki* applies to the people coming from the power ministries (*silovie ministerstva*) such as the Ministry of Internal Affairs or the Ministry of Defense and from power structures (*silovie strukturi*) such as the Federal Security Service (FSB). The term *siloviki* can also refer to a specific "clan" in Russian politics. However, its complete makeup remains a mystery. *Silovoki* as a group are undoubtedly more heterogeneous than homogeneous. But the inability to distinguish the institutional origins of actors described as *siloviki* is part of the problem in analyzing the distribution of power. The mere notion of *siloviki* is highly debatable and should be clarified. In this book, the notion is limited to people coming from power ministries and power structures, which include:

- Ministry of Foreign Affairs (MID)
- Ministry of Justice (*MinYust*)
- Ministry of Internal Affairs (MVD)
- Ministry for Civil Defense, Emergency Situations, and Disaster Relief (MChS)
- Ministry of Defense (MO)
- Federal Security Service (FSB)
- Federal Border Service (FPS)
- Foreign Intelligence Service (SVR)
- Federal Protection Service (FSO)
- Federal Customs Service (FTS)
- Federal Drug Control Service (FSKN)
- Main Directorate for Special Programs (GUSP)
- Presidential Directorate for Administrative Affairs (UDPRF)

The issue of the *siloviki* certainly invites scrutiny of Putin's methods for reinforcing his own power: To what extent has he relied on the *siloviki* as a whole or on different groups that were completely or partly staffed by former colleagues from the intelligence services or the office of the mayor of St. Petersburg? In terms of operating, to what extent have Putin and members of his inner circle used "international terrorism" as an excuse to centralize power? A lot has been said and written about the *siloviki*, implying that they are responsible for the trend toward conservatism and the centralization of power. This vision of a conspiracy is widespread both in Russia and abroad. On the other hand, one can argue that the personalized nature of power as well as the way in which Yeltsin dealt with—or more precisely did not deal with—civil-military relations could have induced a sort of political vacuum that people prepared to protect the regime—whoever its leader—felt compelled to fill.

In this context, the appointment of Sergey Ivanov as the first "civilian" minister of defense in March 2001 and his promotion to deputy prime minister in November 2005 were significant developments, given that he hails from the intelligence services and at one time was seen as a possible successor to Putin. After he advanced to first deputy prime minister in February 2007, Anatoly Serdyukov became minister of defense. Such a succession of "civilian" defense ministers is particularly significant. Conversely, another question deserves to be raised: Did the desire for reform on the part of Putin and his defense minister come up against inertia and division within the security community? Was this inertia combined with apathy for military matters on the part of the civilian elite and the public? These questions are all the more pertinent because, officially, military reform had been completed in October 2003.

For these reasons, this book concentrates on three pivotal aspects of the relationship between the civil and military spheres: a sort of "sociology" of power at the highest level of the state; decision-making methods resulting in the use of force; and *derzhavnichestvo*'s impact on the Kremlin's international ambitions. However, this book is not an academic study of the security community as such or a thorough analysis of its doctrine. This book will refrain from dealing with larger issues such as Russian security policy and military reform. The study is empirical and descriptive in its approach and is based on a large set of interviews conducted in Moscow with politicians, officers, officials, and experts between January 2005 and September 2007.

In short, this work aims to understand the very informal and rather unpredictable nature of civil-military relations in Russia and the consequent organization of power, which under Medvedev and beyond will certainly remain in constant flux. This combination of the informal and the unpredictable, which is so characteristic of the Russian system, helps explain many of the misunderstandings between Russia and other nations.

It is precisely the relationship between Russia and other nations that justifies this policy-oriented examination. Because of its assertiveness, Russia is seen as rejecting so-called Western standards of development. Relying on its own capabilities, Russia officially intends to control both the time frame and the form of its development. This position leads many observers to fear a resurgent Russia with the potential to once again be a direct military threat to the West. This book does not support that view even if risks certainly exist.

Observing Russia from Europe, it is always highly sensitive to focus on the links between Russia and its neighbors. Russia's recent behavior could be interpreted as setting out on a neo-imperialist path, aggressively investing in foreign markets, increasing its military expenditure, seeking to dominate its near abroad. In addition, it is often said that Russia wants to thwart Western influence by driving a wedge between the United States and the European Union, as well as among the EU member states.

Being at war and having regained world-power status partly through energy, Russia has entered a phase of unexpected economic expansion and political assertiveness. Part of the international concern about Russia is whether this trend could result in stable relations, and whether Russia would eventually accept the constraints of global market conventions. Essentially, Russia needs to avoid direct confrontation. However, the Russian leadership will face the tensions inherent in pursuing a policy charted between aggressive promotion of Russia's interests and the desire to be seen as a reliable partner.

In the Western conception of international relations, there is a sort of *doxa* that holds that an undemocratic regime is a threat not only to its own society and neighbors, but also to its partners. The general assumption is quite well known: The strengthening of internal, domestic power will, sooner or later, translate into the strengthening of external power. In this view, being—by Western standards—abnormal politically, economically, and strategically, Russia is not able to pursue a predictable foreign policy.

Difficulties establishing partnerships on the Russian side and difficulties empathizing with Russia on the Western side can largely be explained by the divergence in the two sides' concepts of how to balance civil and military interests. Russian analysis on the topic concentrates on the means of reacting to a system of threats and maintaining the integrity of the state. Western analysis concentrates on the democratization process with the clear subordination of the military and the security services to civilian power. In the euphoria of the transition years, the Russian concept of civil-military relations was supposed to become similar to the Western one. It is time to accept that this has not been the case and to anticipate the consequences.

CHAPTER ONE

The Heritage of Civil-Military
Relations in Russia

In Russia, the relationship between the civil and military spheres extends into the organization of power. While not necessarily agreeing with each other, Western analysts use common theoretical models and historical patterns for exploring this topic. Usually, the relationship in postcommunist Russia is analyzed "from the perspective of democratic standards"[1] and therefore is seen as a gauge of the democratization process.

The theoretical models based on democratization may prove to be inappropriate, while at the same time can be understood as ideal types through which the Russian leaders reach or avoid Western standards. Studying these models helps to establish what is at stake, while bearing in mind the effect they have on our understanding of reality. Even if reality never definitively concurs with models, they are essential to clarify the distribution of power. Yet caution is in order: Rather than conducting an exhaustive analysis of the different models, it is more useful to retain those that clarify the current situation and pave the way for reflection, while simultaneously examining the connection between civil-military relations reform and democratic transition on the one hand, and between balancing that relationship with operational efficiency, on the other.[2]

In this context, historical patterns refer to the ideas, symbols, and behaviors of the past. They are strong habits deeply rooted in strategic culture. This psychological baggage cannot be avoided, and it influences—consciously or subconsciously—any type of leadership. There is no Russian specificity from this point of view, except that this heritage is largely based on the traditions of militarism. That is why it is often described by Western experts as a barrier to Russia's democratization process.[3] This heritage should nevertheless be given serious consideration if we want to understand the current Russian mind-set. This is of high importance for Vladimir Putin, who during his two terms as president acted according to historical patterns. His obsession with *prestige* clearly stems from this heritage. For the purpose of analysis, it would not be sensible to disconnect theoretical models from historical patterns and ignore Russian traditions in favor of blindly using the Western ideal types. Putin's legacy in civil-military relations is much more the result of Russian history than of external attempts to make the Russian leadership change its power structures. For Putin, the major task was dealing with both the Soviet legacy and the Yeltsin legacy. Whether it will be easier for his successor Medvedev is an open question.

Models of Civil-Military Relations

The need for models and patterns can also be explained by a personal experience. As I conducted interviews in Moscow on the topic of civil-military relations, it was striking to hear very divergent interpretations of the same concept. For instance, the concept of "civilian control" is essential to describe a model that respects the key democratic principle of the military's subordination to civilian power. In Russia, this concept (*grazhdanskiy kontrol*) is understood in very different ways. One general officer and member of *Yedinaya Rossiya* (United Russia, the presidential party) in the State Duma sums it up as "the president's control of nuclear arms." One expert has added that this concept is relevant only in the West, because in Russia no clear distinction exists between the political and military spheres. This last expert also emphasized that "civil control" is not a widespread notion in Russia and that it would be understood in Western terms only by a small number of specialists. In terms of historical patterns, many officers and officials often refer to the Great Patriotic War to describe the role of institutional actors such as the General Staff. More broadly, the Second World War and its subsequent political exploitation are central in the current perception of civil-military relations. The experience of the war under Stalin's leadership remains haunting in terms of controlling the military by ensuring strict discipline and absolute loyalty to the state at all levels.[4] Through interviews, it appears that the Russian elite—much more than its counterparts in Europe and in the United States—looks to the past as a way of understanding the present and the future in military affairs.

Balancing civil and military institutions has been at the heart of political philosophy since antiquity. How is it possible to guard the guards? For Plato, the city was based on four cardinal virtues: wisdom, courage, temperance, and justice. Wisdom was held by the leaders and spread through them to the entire community. Courage was the virtue held by the leaders' auxiliaries, that is, the guards of city dogma and territory; the city would be renowned as courageous or not depending on the guards' value. The political structure was thus based on a fundamental distinction between those two groups and on the principle by which the majority was protected by a clearly identified minority.

Regardless of the regime and era, the civil-military balance tends to be restricted to the issue of military intervention and military dictatorship, that is, to the use of force in ruling a city by those responsible for protecting it. This approach is too restrictive, even in regard to Russia, where the threat of force was frequently raised, and even used, for both internal and external purposes at the beginning of the transition period. This threat is invoked much less often today. Some analysts believe that it cannot be fully done away with, given that the loyalty of Russian armed forces has never been truly tested.[5] Others, by contrast, believe that this threat, and the fear it engenders, is largely the result of myth.[6]

The attempted coup against Soviet President Mikhail Gorbachev in August 1991 has taught us much in this regard. Stirred up by a group comprising the head of the KGB, the minister of defense, the minister of the interior, and the prime minister, this coup failed because of the military High Command's refusal to resort to force. For the High Command, it was less a matter of countering the insurgents than of maintaining a position of referee and avoiding the use of force against civilians at all costs. The "Tbilisi syndrome" (named for troops' resentment over being ordered to open fire in April 1989 to suppress demonstrations) can also explain the armed forces' reluctance in executing missions to maintain order.[7]

This framework must be extended beyond a possible coup. In practice, rules governing the relationship between civil and military institutions cannot be limited to preparing for an impromptu eruption of violence; the daily running of a democracy demands that the two be regulated, if not harmonious. Indeed, the relationship affects the division of responsibility between civilians and the military in times of war and in the event of restricted interventions, but most of all in times of peace. What, after all, is the use of force and, consequently, those who wield it, if the primary political objective is to not make use of it? The difficulty of being part of the armed forces in times of peace, in Russia as elsewhere, must never be forgotten.

Beyond the central issue of determining who holds the monopoly on legitimate violence, deciding how to balance the civil and military spheres is important, according to Eliot A. Cohen, in at least six areas of public action: the stature of the armed forces in government; the definition of criteria for the use of force; the creation of military forces adapted to the chosen missions; the mobilization and relation with civil society; the proportion of funds designated for the armed forces from public spending (most often discretionary); and the drawing up of foreign policy.[8]

Reflections on civil-military relations remain largely influenced by Samuel P. Huntington's seminal work.[9] It provides "the language and concepts of civil-military relations" from which the models deployed in the United States and Europe stem.[10] This language and these concepts are worth applying to the Russian situation, while bearing in mind that doing so remains an attempt to project an external model on a particular case. On this topic the United States clearly dominates the intellectual debate. This fact is due as much to the bipolar confrontation of the Cold War (which guided a great number of academic works) as to the Soviet Union's poor theoretical thinking during that period (and whose thinking was not remedied thereafter).[11] Huntington has described a model for civilian control based on four fundamental principles:

- The nature of the military involves a high degree of professionalism as well as recognition of the limits of this professional competence by military authorities—an intrinsically problematic issue.
- The military must accept subordination to civil political leaders who make the essential decisions on foreign policy and security. This principle of subordination does not address the issue of the degree of expertise needed by political decision makers in security matters.
- The political elite must recognize and accept the armed forces' specific competence and the need to grant them professional autonomy. Such recognition does not resolve the issue concerning the degree of autonomy required for broader equilibrium in civil-military relations.
- The involvement of the armed forces in the political sphere and, conversely, the involvement of the political elite in the military sphere should be limited. Involvement may be relatively sustainable and binding. Nevertheless, the limitation implies a sufficiently responsive interaction.

These general principles reveal the balance of civil and military relations to be like an equation. It means that the political leadership—despite subordinating military power—should respect a set of conditions for this subordination to be effective. Huntington moreover reminds us that, as far as new democracies are concerned, difficulties in terms of civil-military relations often arise from the civilian control side of the equation, especially when that side fails to promote economic development and ensure the rule of law.[12] The division of civilian control and military power should therefore always be related to the country's politico-economic situation and sociocultural context, and should not be seen as a self-enclosed and disconnected entity. Civilian control and military power are, in fact, very dependent on the national context and the international environment. This is particularly true in the Russian context. It is useful to consider these general principles and the situation in Russia to understand that during the Yeltsin years civil-military relations far from followed the model put forth by Samuel Huntington. Given the fact that Yeltsin "was not interested in the armed forces," he created an incomplete presidential leadership that affected the High Command.[13] When Putin acceded to power, he had to deal with this vacuum.

During the Yeltsin period, the Russian armed forces exuded inefficiency rather than professionalism.[14] Moreover, they appeared to be territorial defense forces rather than forces to be deployed abroad.[15] Despite some operations that had limited success, the post-Soviet Russian forces have accumulated setbacks and seem to have snatched defeat from the jaws of victory.

Historical Patterns

Since the seventeenth century, Russia has conceived its strategy with three geographic theaters in mind: the west (from the Baltic to the Carpathians), the south (from the Danube to the mountains of Persia), and the east (from the Volga to the Altay).[16] The Russian leadership has always sought the ability to intervene simultaneously in these three theaters. The will to conserve this flexibility at all costs resulted in a mode of power organization characterized by a single command unit (the czar and his advisers) and a ruling class dominated by the military. This system entailed a very close association between the *prestige* of the state and that of the military for the population and the elite. In the imperial era, as in the Soviet era, military objectives prevailed over everything else. This fundamental militarism was also manifest in the fear of encirclement, rooted not only in the memories of Mongol domination in the thirteenth and fourteenth centuries but also in attempted invasions from the west. This spatial configuration explains the "hard core" of Russian strategic thinking, which, as a consequence, consists of carrying out massive attacks deep in hostile territory.[17] From a historical point of view, Russian strategy has struggled to conceive action without vast theaters of operation and without the capacity to strike from a distance.

Obviously, bipolar confrontation has been the object of extensive analyses by Western experts on the balance between civil and military institutions. Such analyses had to understand the nature of relations between the Communist Party and the military in the USSR in order to define the objectives of Moscow's security policy, and to identify the politico-military connections in the system susceptible of being targeted in times of conflict. In Soviet times, military power was cherished for three main reasons: supporting territorial expansion; maintaining order within the communist bloc; and always being ready to defend the *rodina* (motherland).[18] There is no need to reproduce this literature in its entirety, but merely to review the main interpretations of Soviet civil-military relations, to clarify the similarities between the Soviet model (which is more ambiguous than previously presented) and the post-Soviet situation.

Studies by Roman Kolkowicz marked a significant step forward in assessing civil-military relations in the Soviet era.[19] Following in the footsteps of Samuel Huntington, he perceived the relationship as a zero-sum game and regarded the military as an institution closed in on itself. He believed that the Soviet military claimed professional autonomy in the name of efficiency. The Communist Party, for its part, was categorically opposed to the military's autonomy and advocated instead infiltration of the military by party leaders in order to exercise close ideological control. The party believed it had the right and above all the duty to become involved in military affairs in the name of its predominant ideology. This situation fueled permanent tension between civil and military powers: The gain of one seemed to come at the other's expense.

Subsequently, this conception of civil-military relations as a zero-sum game was strongly criticized by William E. Odom.[20] He proposed a more sociological understanding, whereby the civil and military powers were interchangeable in the Soviet Union. Odom argued that the civilian and military spheres shared the same values and had a common interest in maintaining the system; in this respect, if conflicts do arise, they are controlled due to the standardization of bureaucracy and ideology.

Timothy J. Colton and Thane Gustafson, for their part, have attempted to synthesize these two approaches.[21] They believe that Kolkowicz overestimated the control exercised by the Communist Party. At the same time, they considered Odom to be mistaken in having assimilated the civil and military spheres via bureaucratic normalization. According to them, the post-1989 military retained a considerable level of autonomy over the essential aspects of its activities: discipline, promotion, operational training—at least on a tactical level—and, not least, combat. Colton and Gustafson proposed a model for the interaction of the civil elite and the military, whereby neither side could exert absolute dominance over the other. However, both sides accepted the party's sovereign power. This approach resulted in a confrontation/cooperation model between the two sides, the intensity of which depends on the circumstances. These debates are definitely useful in interpreting the discourse of today's main players.

Kolkowicz's interpretation of civil-military relations as being a zero-sum game permeates the discourse of experts close to the Kremlin, who emphasize the stabilization carried out in recent years. It is opposed by experts critical of Putin in two ways. The first argument is that the game is limited today because, despite official statements to the contrary, political power remains mostly inactive. The second argument shifts the point of view, placing the real focus not so much on the civilian-military balance but on the present state of society and its scant understanding of military affairs.

Odom's ideological stance is found, indirectly, in James H. Billington's discourse highlighting just how far Russia has come in being "de-ideologized." Such a process would result in such a profound lack of identity, Billington contends, that it could result in social disintegration if this vacuum is not quickly filled by the search for common and federalizing values.[22]

Colton and Gustafson's confrontation/cooperation model has been taken up by a number of people who emphasize the immense difficulties currently encountered by civil and military authorities in agreeing upon a definition of national interests. Confrontation is primarily found in the definition of threats and management of capabilities, that is, for those who adhere to "military doctrine"; cooperation is more understood as a lack of conflict, and hence the status quo. The Russian interpretation of "military doctrine" (*voennaya doktrina*)—a key notion that does not conform to Western understanding—corresponds to the sociopolitical environment in which a conflict arises. It involves drawing up scenarios and predicting useful methods, but it does not touch upon the use of force. This, in Russian strategic thinking, corresponds with the doctrine of operational art (*operativnoe iskusstvo*).[23]

The Civil-Military Balance and the Fall of the USSR

After the fall of the USSR, the balance between the civil and military spheres came under close scrutiny, particularly by Western experts, who saw the possibility of recasting the balance during the transition. Indeed, civil-military relations have since been incorporated into a global approach to democratic transition and the necessary means for carrying it out. This approach tends to disassociate the civil and military spheres from purely strategic ones, meaning that they are considered more from a legal viewpoint. In this respect, the civil-military relationship is based on three principles: the imposition of firm, prescriptive constraints on political involvement in the army; clear and legal distribution of responsibility between civil and military institutions; and—what is most crucial in the Russian case—a clear distinction between traditional armed forces and other structures responsible for state-sanctioned violence.[24] This theoretical approach, understood and supported by the liberal wing of Russia's strategic community (a core group of high-quality but politically marginalized experts), is rapidly heading toward ambivalent super-presidentialism and apathy in the security community.

What is obvious today was not necessarily so obvious in the euphoria of the transition's outset—that, unlike in former Warsaw Pact satellites or newly independent states of the former Soviet Union, the balance of civil and military institutions in Russia could not be rebuilt in the same way.[25] Russia was neither a NATO candidate nor a nascent state. This fact calls for a new analysis of civil-military relations in the Soviet era to better understand the underlying effects these relations will have on the structure of the military. Such an analysis would allow for a better understanding of the workings of a system that primarily has to be broken down and then built back up again, following the general principles of an ideal type largely inspired by Western models. In this field, as in others, progression and regression are measured against a prevailing intellectual design from abroad. These foreign views are not all in accord. Instead, they provoke rejection and tension associated with the troubled identity of a Russia unable to assimilate its imperial past. Whether in the czarist era or the Soviet era, the military is the beginning, the middle, and, to a certain extent, the end of the Russian project. In this respect, the military cannot be separated from the world's relation to Russia and is inevitably under strain, both in times of declining Russian power (such as in the 1990s) and in times of consolidation (such as now). In Russia, more than anywhere else, there is no doubt that tensions between civil and military institutions are at the heart of the political system and the prism through which foreign policy is largely formulated.

Believing that none of the three schools of thought previously mentioned fully appreciate the complexity of the civil-military balance in the Soviet system, Dale R. Herspring proposed a chronological approach to show how precarious this balance was.[26] To Herspring, the two sides are never fixed. According to him, the civil and military spheres were in conflict at the start of the 1930s because of the Communist Party's proclaimed will to dominate the entire military sphere. The party's staunch determination to submit the military to its will is clearly manifest in that era, with the intent of attaining (via Stalin's purges, which destroyed any vague attempt at autonomy) an ideologically homogeneous and docile military. The Great Patriotic War naturally changed the balance of power, but it was not until after Stalin's death in March 1953 that the armed forces could begin emerging from their subjection. They managed to regain autonomy in certain areas, such as in the "operational doctrine" and the organization of forces. Under the cooperative climate during the regimes of Nikita Khrushchev and Leonid Brezhnev, civil-military relations improved, leading some analysts to refer to the Soviet High Command under Brezhnev as "golden age," during which time it managed to obtain almost all the resources it wanted.[27]

The Soviet invasion of Afghanistan in December 1979 ruptured this fragile balance. The militarization of the regime was felt in the overdevelopment of the military-industrial complex, the overproduction of military equipment, and the disconnection of security challenges from available resources. The failure in Afghanistan had its roots in Russia's strategic mind-set based on a frontal approach, the delimitation of theaters on an operative level, and large-scale attacks that were ill-adapted to the terrain and the mobility of the Afghan resistance. Eighty-five percent of the Soviet forces were used to provide basic security; consequently, only 15 percent of the forces were available to pursue the mujahideen.[28] What is more, the Soviet forces suffered from a doctrinal shortfall. The General Staff was unable to provide a counterinsurgency strategy because of their ideologically-based assumption that only capitalist countries could be involved in local wars.[29] (A few years later in Chechnya, very little operational information on asymmetric warfare had been assimilated from the painful Afghan experience, which highlights the Russian forces' poor capacity for learning or self-appraisal.)[30] The invasion of Afghanistan subsequently met with a double defeat, military and political. In retrospect, this campaign was indicative of a deep fracture. Confusion between ideological and regional objectives accelerated the regime's downfall, while permanently traumatizing the armed forces, the effects of which were felt not only in purely military terms but also in relations with civilian power. This deep trauma (which could be compared to the trauma of Vietnam in the United States, or of Algeria in France) has affected a generation of officers and was soon followed by the collapse of the USSR and the dissolution of the Warsaw Pact. Defeated in Afghanistan, this generation had to deal with the aftermath. For many of them, it corresponded with a strong deterioration of their standard of living as well as a decline of their status in a fast-moving society.

When he came to power in the mid-1980s, Mikhail Gorbachev attempted to restrict the autonomy of the armed forces, which was by then far more extensive than that of their Western counterparts. He came up against both the entrenched privileges of the military in society and the delicate issue of managing conscription.[31] Gorbachev believed that control of the military—in particular for drawing up the doctrine and organizing forces—had to be regained to limit both budgetary slides and the militarization of the economy. All this needed to be achieved while imposing a new conceptual framework for foreign policy in Moscow. By quitting the arms race and making disarmament the main focus of policy vis-à-vis the Western bloc, Gorbachev reversed the regime's order of priorities. Indeed, he refused to allocate large-scale resources to the military.

The army subsequently played a double role in the attempted coup against Gorbachev in August 1991: Some units participated, while the majority's inertia contributed to the coup's failure.[32] From August 1991 on, Boris Yeltsin granted some increased autonomy to the armed forces, but thereafter gradually attempted to tighten his control by using the budget, the parliament, and the media. These attempts did not, however, mean the end of military operations: Despite its international weakness, Russia under Yeltsin increased its military involvement in the CIS before setting out, totally unprepared, for the first Chechnya campaign.

This historical overview led Herspring to emphasize the delicate nature of the three factors in particular: "military doctrine" (which regulates the perception and definition of threat); army design (which implies deciding between a large conscript army and a reduced professional tool); and career management (which calls for a clear definition of criteria for promotion as well as the extent to which outside interference in military appointments is permitted). At all times, these three factors reflect the state of the civilian-military balance.

Civil-Military Relations in Post-Soviet Russia

Taking these three factors into account may seem obvious to Western analysts, who today tend to advocate a broader approach to civil-military relations by "reforming the security sector." It is not so obvious in a post-Soviet Russia marked by a series of political and economic setbacks and by the fragmentation of the armed forces and security. There is little sense in considering this fragmentation as an isolated phenomenon, for it is an integral part of an extremely chaotic political context.[33] It is explained, first of all, by the hybrid nature of the system set up by Boris Yeltsin, namely, a super-presidential, institutional regime on the one hand, and a leader whose capacity for action is weakened, on the other. It is also explained by the large social and regional disparities between different ranks of officers and by the experience of war: The importance of experience goes a long way in explaining the popularity of General Alexander Lebed, who relentlessly denounced the engagement of troops in Chechnya by generals unaccustomed to the cost or taste of blood.[34] What is more, the fragmentation of forces was heightened by tension with the security services, over which Yeltsin attempted to gain control from the outset. This fragmentation would thus be both the cause, and consequence, of the breakdown in officers' morale.[35]

This overview has so far not taken into account the interpretations made by the community of Russian experts, in which Andrey A. Kokoshin has distinguished himself.[36] As a practitioner and analyst,[37] Kokoshin has emphasized historical legacy for understanding civil-military relations. According to him, the idea of reforming the relationship involved a fundamental rupture from the Soviet heritage. A new realist approach to understanding the relationship would entail taking into account three factors: the Russian military heritage; the development in Soviet strategic thinking; and the lessons to be drawn from the Soviet Union's "super-militarism." Kokoshin has also called for a better understanding of the essence of Soviet doctrine, recalling that all reforms of the relationship between civil and military institutions are bound up with reflections on Russian identity—which includes the identification of national interests—and carry profound consequences. Another decisive element, with which Kokoshin has personally struggled, is the military-industrial complex, which benefited from a great deal of autonomy during Yeltsin's administration. The military-industrial complex uses this autonomy to promote its own interests, affecting the balance of the civil-military relationship.

At the same time, Alexei G. Arbatov (president of the Defense Committee of the State Duma from 1994 to 2003 and vice president of *Yabloko*, one of the Russian liberal parties), took a much more radical stance by emphasizing the urgency of decisions that had to be made.[38] To highlight the seriousness of the situation, Arbatov drew a parallel between Soviet Russia's situation in 1941 and that of the Russian Federation in 1998. He also argued that military reform was crucial for all reforms yet to come, while linking the inability to reform to increased anti-Western sentiment. An additional element, which proved to be key under Vladimir Putin, is that military reform must affect not only the Ministry of Defense but also all security organizations. Kokoshin and Arbatov are still debating. Kokoshin has proposed a broad reflection on Russia's strategic conduct, fueled by historical analysis and a comparative approach.[39] Arbatov thinks that despite its attempts at reform, Russia currently has a military apparatus that is the opposite of its strategic needs.[40]

In his very fine analysis of institutions and bureaucracy, Kokoshin dwelled on the many consequences of the regime's strong "presidentialization" in terms of balancing civil and military institutions. Presidentialization is felt less in the major strategic orientations of the security community than in the appointments made within the High Command or the security services. The appointments are the main instruments available to the Kremlin for altering the institutional balance. In practice, however, the appointments have limited capacity for transformation. Arbatov, for his part, emphasized the necessity of rethinking both the coordination among different security organizations and the articulation of the foreign and security policies. This approach assumed a series of measures: maximum transparency of the defense budget; an increase in this budget; a 50 percent reduction in the number of troops by 2010; a sense of professionalization; a net increase in equipment; a revision of the nuclear doctrine; the creation of compact, mobile, and coordinated units; and, finally, an overall strategic reorientation, making local conflicts top priority.

These proposals seem far removed from reality. In fact, over the course of the 1990s, the balance of the civilian and military institutions in Russia has been caught in a vicious circle over how to achieve stability in a state that is breaking down. During this period, it was impossible to lay the foundations of a new state organization without broaching the nature of civil-military interaction, especially for a former military superpower. This vicious circle would explain the profound degradation of civil-military relations under Yeltsin, who could have contained the situation by offering a carrot (corrupting the High Command) while wielding a stick (reducing the army's size).[41]

Unlike the Russian analysts previously mentioned, several Western analysts believe that the main difficulties today lie on the civilian side of the equation.[42] Using a comparative method (Poland, Hungary, Ukraine, and Russia), David Betz has highlighted two key elements in the development of the civil-military balance since the fall of the USSR that would be the conditions for success: the prospect of joining NATO and the potential for softening the Russian elite's attitude. In Russia's case, NATO's transformations, and successive enlargements, were certainly big turnoffs for a defense system conceived and maintained precisely in the event of a showdown with NATO. This incentive was clearly counterproductive. As far as the elite are concerned, neither the civilian nor the military sphere was interested in creating democratic-style reform: The president was duty-bound to have a politically neutral army contributing to his political survival, while the High Command found that the safest means of safeguarding its budget was by establishing personal relations with the Kremlin. Moreover, Betz has encouraged the shift from the traditional civilian-military paradigm, based on a deep-seated rivalry between the two sides, to an integration paradigm that, according to him, is an issue of public administration management rather than civil control.

This paradigm of integration, while avoiding confrontation, calls back (whether consciously or unconsciously) to that of civil-military fusion. This is manifest by a disproportion between the army's structure and available resources while maintaining a latent militarism, that is, a social overvaluation of the military, which was, of course, where Russian absolutism and Soviet communism obtained their legitimacy.[43] The civil-military fusion was certainly one of the main characteristics of Putin's leadership. Compared to Yeltsin, he showed his "impassioned love" for the military and created a sort of "civilian militarism."[44] At a deeper level, Putin used the military's symbols to reinforce its own power. From his point of view, the Russian armed forces and security services are by nature heroic; several times in the history of the Russian state, they were its savior. That is why Putin always emphasized the *prestige* of the security community to legitimize its own power and to feed Russia's resurgent patriotism. This last point is important to note: After the years of humiliation associated with the Yeltsin period, Putin wanted to restore honor and pride to the Russian people. In terms of political communication, the security community without doubt was his most practical tool.

Using a historical point of view, Russian analysts consider that the state was founded on the army. Consequently, the elite would naturally be tainted by this fusion and the congenital interweaving of political and military interests. Alexander M. Golts has argued that Russia lost precious years through the unsuccessful modification of its defense system and civil-military relations.[45] This incapacity is rooted in the Russo–Soviet strategic culture. According to Golts, the failure of military reform since the fall of the USSR cannot be explained by a lack of consensus over the nature of reform, the fear of military influence over internal political debates, a lack of financial resources, or the conflict in Chechnya (nor can it be explained by a combination of these factors). It can, however, according to Golts, be explained by three historic facts. First, the Russian people and the elite associate the *prestige* of the state with military *prestige*. Indeed, in both the imperial and Soviet eras, military objectives took precedence over other objectives. Second, the Russian military benefits from a degree of administrative and operational autonomy that has no equivalent in Western armies. The security services enjoy even greater autonomy. Consequently, the ability of governmental authorities to impose their views is limited. Third, the militarism that characterizes Russian society is deeply embedded in serfdom and autocracy. The successes of the Russo–Soviet armed forces reinforce the authority of the state and its legitimacy to demand sacrifices from the population.[46] In his analysis, Golts rejects historical determinism, believing that Russian authorities could have opted for different organizational choices at each stage of Russia's politico-military development. The weight of the past led Golts to advocate a complete modification of history taught to the Russian elite and the creation of an alternative system for military training by means of civilian-run establishments. The need to give officers more than a purely military education is generally not recognized in Russia,[47] and precisely this lack of a broader education severely complicates exchanges between Russian and Western armed forces.

This brief overview demonstrates the importance that historical patterns have on the leadership's behavior. In contrast with Yeltsin, Putin, who had a limited political base when he took power, understood perfectly that the politico-military balance was the best means of legitimizing his own power. His personal interest was definitely genuine, given his background, but there was also a conscious political reason for identifying military *prestige* with himself and his presidency. To understand the evolution from Yeltsin to Putin, five points deserve to be highlighted.

First, civilian-military relations are not governed by fate. Neither side—civilian nor military—is favored over the other; instead, they reflect a balance that is highly dependent on the political context. It is thus necessary to pay close attention to the current political situation, which, under Putin, was undoubtedly more fluid than the super-presidentialism thesis would have us believe. Politically, Putin remained weak during the first years of his tenure. Little by little, he became tougher and emerged from his first term as a very cautious reformer. His reelection in 2004 gave him the political resources to modify civil-military relations, or at least establish a new balance. Political context cannot be understood without a clear vision of the fast-moving economic situation since 2000. In reality, the main rupture is an economic one, insofar as Putin benefited from a much more favorable financial situation than his predecessor, with cumulated growth in gross domestic product of more than 55 percent from 1999 to 2007, versus a decline in GDP of 44 percent from 1989 to 1998. For the first time since the collapse of the USSR, the Russian leadership was in a position to allocate new financial resources.

Second, just as the *afgantsy*—the veterans who returned from the Afghan war—influenced the beginning of the post-Soviet transition period, the question naturally arises as to the influence officers who served in Chechnya might have today. Military experience on the ground inevitably serves as the backdrop to any reform attempts. For an army, what is most important is actual combat: battles fought, won or lost. From this perspective, the two wars in Chechnya (1994–1996, 1999–2007) lie at the heart of the politico-military divide, and they represent another key psychological factor too often ignored: Since the collapse of the USSR, political authorities and armed forces have become strangers to the notion of victory. This lack of success deprives them of the cement that is internal cohesion, and it weakens their *prestige* abroad. The two Chechnya campaigns also reveal that the broader objective of Moscow's strategic tradition—namely, preserving the country's territorial integrity at all costs—is still very much alive. Russian officers and experts also make a clear distinction between the first and the second wars, purely in military terms. Irrespective of the methods used, the second war is seen both as a victory and revenge for the security community, especially since Shamil Basayev, one of the most famous leaders of the Chechnya separatist movement, was killed in July 2006. Even if the situation remains unstable, limited triumphs are crucial to the security community's self-esteem and its attitude toward the political leadership.

Third, the issue of civilian and military relations is not limited to relations between those two spheres. In addition to incorporating the military-industrial complex, it should include all security organs—and that is precisely where the field's main research difficulty lies. Indeed, the problem is twofold: grasping the institutional postures in relation to one another while bearing in mind the highly informal nature of their relations with the Kremlin. One Russian expert has stated, with a touch of irony, that a shrewd knowledge of the "*banya* factor" (the baths) should be the ultimate objective of all research in the field. In other words, behind-the-scenes elements remain crucial—if highly difficult—for any external researcher to grasp. However, in terms of methodology, any research on civil and military institutions and how they interact in Russia, as elsewhere, requires consistent attention to "informal procedures, routines, norms and conventions."[48] Once again, it involves the careful consideration of Russian strategic culture.

Fourth, David Betz's comparative approach usefully recalled that the development of the civil-military balance can never be disassociated from geopolitical positioning and, consequently, the system of alliances. From this perspective, the framework that NATO endorses may serve both as a role model (Poland, Hungary) and as a counter-model (Russia). In this respect, Ukraine has an ambivalent position accentuated by the Orange Revolution that swept President Viktor Yushchenko to power. The enlargement of NATO has clearly left an indelible mark on the development of Russia's political and military spheres.

Finally, the debate over the merging of the civil authority and the military is part of an approach that makes Russia an anomaly in Western eyes. It is closely linked to the debate over specificity and notably was used by Putin to justify certain measures (a point we will come back to). Already, historical interpretations of state-military relations in Russia seem to contribute directly to the elaboration of a model unique to Russia.

The Security Community in the Balance of Power

Russian defense expenditure nearly quadrupled during the past six years, resulting in definite improvements in the welfare of the security community. Thus, Western perceptions of the capabilities and living conditions of the Russian armed forces may be outdated. In such circumstances, the challenge remains to assess the real state of the security community in terms of power distribution.

Compared to the Yeltsin era, the Kremlin's supremacy in decision making on foreign and security policies was indisputably reinforced under Putin.[1] However, during Putin's first term, the presence of influential groups, such as the "Chechen generals" (Konstantin Pulikovsky, Gennady Troshev, Viktor Kazantsev, Vladimir Shamanov, and—until he was ousted—Anatoly Kvashnin) resulted in the High Command's making decisions that, in theory, should have been the sole responsibility of the president. Part of Putin's challenge was deciding whether to tolerate or reject this kind of influence. On a broader note, the security community remained a key actor in the framing of foreign and security policy, especially its nuclear and industrial aspects. What about under Putin? Did the security community continue to directly influence the trajectory of Russian foreign policy in regard to nuclear disarmament, nonproliferation, and export controls? At the same time, did it exert strong influence over relations among CIS countries through regional security structures, such as the Collective Security Treaty Organization (which, in addition to Russia, consists of Armenia, Belarus, Kazakhstan, Kyrgyzstan, and Tajikistan)?

Under Yeltsin, the autonomy of the armed forces contributed to their marginalization. Indeed, the forces seemed to be a closed entity, cut off from society, despite the conscription system that makes conscripts and their families

completely dependent on the institution. They also appeared to be an institution the political leadership found impossible to deal with, since they were
geared not toward operational efficiency, but toward preserving a mode of
organization that defended its corporate interests. In other words, during the
1990s, "autonomy" was synonymous with corporatism.

In retrospect, Yeltsin neither controlled nor regulated interaction between
the civilian and military spheres. Many former military personnel were
involved in the country's political life at a number of levels. Conversely, initiatives stemming from the civil leadership intended to influence the military
sphere were limited, owing notably to the lack of expertise in the civil community. This situation has led some analysts to suggest that the main source
of control exerted on the armed forces came from the Committee of Soldiers'
Mothers, a human rights organization.

In this context, Putin was faced with three challenges: the design of the
security community, its disunity, and its control.

Overall Design of the Security Community[2]

Ministry of Defense (MO)   1,027,000
- Ground forces
- Air forces
- Naval forces
- Strategic dissuasion forces
- Rail troops
- Special construction troops
- Aerospace forces

Ministry of Internal Affairs (MVD)   821,000
- Internal troops   200,000
- Special Forces (Spetsnaz – OMON & OMSN)   27,000

Federal Security Service (FSB)   350,000
- Federal Border Service (FPS)   160,000
- Special Forces units   4,000

Ministry for Civil Defense, Emergency Situations,   262,000
and Disaster Relief (MChS)
- Civil defense troops   20,000
- State Fire Service   220,000

Federal Customs Service (FTS)	61,300
Procuracy	53,000
Federal Drug Control Service (FSKN)	33,000
Federal Protection Service (FSO)	10,000–30,000
Main Directorate for Special Programs (GUSP)	
Presidential Directorate for Administrative Affairs (UDPRF)	

To this list it would be appropriate to add the Presidential Security Service (in theory, the SBP is subordinated to the FSO, or *Federalnaya Sluzhba Ohrany*, which is responsible for protecting officials, including at the regional level, but in reality it is broadly autonomous) and the Foreign Intelligence Service (*Sluzhba Vneshney Razvedki*, or SVR, which is responsible for foreign intelligence and is estimated to have a workforce of 15,000). The GRU (*Glavnoe Razvedyvatelnoe Upravlenie*, or Main Intelligence Directorate of the General Staff of the Armed Forces of the Russian Federation) reports to the Ministry of Defense and is responsible for military intelligence.

In March 2003, the border guards were incorporated into the FSB by presidential decree. The FAPSI (or *Federalnoe Agenstvo Pravitelstvennoy Svyazi i Informatsii*), the Federal Agency for Government Communications & Information, which is responsible for electronic intelligence and opinion polls, was split between the Ministry of Defense and the FSB, considerably reinforcing the FSB's weight in the overall system.[3] With approximately 350,000 personnel, the FSB has very broad functions as an intelligence, security, and law enforcement body. It is considered "the big winner" of the March 2003 reorganization. The combined influence of the security services has had a direct impact on the balance between civil and military authority, and it has accentuated discord between the traditional armed forces and the rest of the security community. The security services played a crucial role in the relationship between the civil and military institutions during the Yeltsin period. Their influence under Putin is one of the most debatable parts of his legacy on the relationship. Another actor should be mentioned: the Procuracy under the auspices of the Ministry of Justice. Under Putin, the Procuracy office became a key tool in his fight against the oligarchs, with the power to prosecute. Consequently, the problem is its independence vis-à-vis the political leadership as well as its ability to give instructions to the FSB, both of which are "questionable."[4]

Moreover, it is important to remember that five ministries, five federal services, and two federal agencies are directly dependent on the presidential administration (thereby eluding the control of the prime minister and, to a great extent, the parliament): the Ministry of the Interior; the Ministry of

Civil Defense, Emergency Situations and Eliminations of the Consequences of Natural Disasters (MChS); the Ministry of Foreign Affairs; the Ministry of Defense; and the Ministry of Justice, as well as the postal service, the SVR, the FSB, the antidrug forces and border police, the Directorate for Special Programs, and the Directorate of Presidential Affairs. This point is of particular importance with regard to Medvedev's presidency, and to the fact that Putin has become his prime minister. The relationship between the two men will be tested on their respective links with the security community. Apparently, Medvedev has no real clout in the security field given his background. Paradoxically, this lack of background was the main reason he was chosen over his main challenger, Sergey Ivanov. It remains to be seen whether the prime minister's powers will be redefined by subordinating these ministries, services, and agencies. Is Medvedev ready for this kind of restriction on presidential power? Is Putin ready to give up his position of *primus inter pares* in the security field? These questions illustrate the sensitive nature of civil-military relations in the coming months. The style and ambitions of Medvedev's presidency directly depend on his ability to take the lead in the security field.

Given the strong heterogeneity of the security community, it is hard to imagine that it exerts influence over the political leadership. Nevertheless, the beginning of operations in Chechnya gave the military an opportunity to regain control after years of frustration. In 1999, it was thought that the military's influential capacity depended directly on the success of operations, with the High Command reinforcing its political weight in line with its successes and increasing its demand for additional resources.[5] In this respect, the current situation in Chechnya could be seen as a new situation, in that the Russian army has not been defeated (as it had been in 1996). In addition, a "normalization process" in the political field was achieved and used by the Kremlin as a cover-up for the losses suffered and for regional instability. External observers consider that the role played by Dmitry Kozak, who was put in charge of the Southern Federal District in September 2004, shortly after the Beslan school siege, was decisive. Thanks to him, the future of Chechnya would be thought of in terms of socioeconomic development, not just security.[6] The performance of the Russian military during the second war in Chechnya is evaluated differently by experts and officers interviewed. Some of them believe that the Russian military clearly succeeded in decapitating the Chechen rebellion. Others, however—much more concerned with the methods used by the military—emphasize the operational failures and level of losses, coupled with a depreciation of the entire military. According to them, the failures of the Russian military paradoxically increase its influence on the political leadership, which cannot avoid the consequences of using military power. However, a general feeling has emerged since 2006 that a new era has begun in Chechnya after years of devastation. Irrespective of his past and present behavior, Ramzan Kadyrov (who was just 30 years old when he became president in February 2007) is seen as the only official in Chechnya able to generate initiatives and produce concrete results. His position has been based more on his personal links with Vladimir Putin than on relations with the Russian presidency in general.[7] Herein lies another great uncertainty about Putin's succession: Will Medvedev be able to pursue the paternalist approach that has suited the youthful Kadyrov?

Increases in Security Spending Without Accountability

In terms of allocating financial resources, it is important to note that the security community is certainly the strongest beneficiary of Russia's robust economic growth. The spending boost for "national defense" is one of the principal characteristics of Putin's second term as president.[8] In fact, in August 2004, Putin announced a rise of 40 percent (28 percent accounting for inflation) in the military budget for 2005, an increase of approximately $2.5 billion. In 2005, military expenditure was estimated to total $21 billion, representing 3.9 percent of the Russian GDP. The budget allocated to the armed forces and the security services remains particularly opaque. However, the following trends can be discerned.[9]

From 1992 to 1999, the military budget decreased by 62 percent. After Putin assumed power, security and defense spending increased substantially. Defense spending, which includes the armed forces and scientific research in the defense sector, has more than doubled, from 382 billion rubles in 2000 to 822 billion rubles in 2007 (PPP). The budget for law enforcement organizations such as MVD, Procuracy, and the Ministry of Justice, increased rapidly. For instance, Procuracy's budget increased from 3 billion rubles in 2000 to 27 billion in 2006. Spending per soldier is estimated at $3,800, which is equivalent to a 350 percent increase since 2000.[10] In April 2006, Sergey Ivanov, then minister of defense, trumpeted the doubling of salaries in recent years. Undoubtedly, the living conditions of the officers and troops improved tremendously during Putin's tenure. Even if part of the adjustment was due to economic growth in Russia, there was also a political wish to refurbish the security community after years of social neglect.

It is, however, difficult to know what exactly these figures represent, given the lack of transparency and control over funds.[11] Even though the Duma is close to the Kremlin, many experts note that it is unable to obtain satisfactory information from the Ministry of Defense and other power structures regarding the allocation of resources. The Duma relies on information supplied by the military and has no real right to monitor military spending, which is somewhat embarrassing. One member has stated that "if you ask a member of the defense committee how much a tank costs, he is unable to answer. It is not the committee that controls the army, but the army that controls the committee."

The lack of resources is felt especially among subalterns and soldiers who come from the less-favored classes. According to the units and garrisons, the increase in the military budget continues to mask the precariousness of their social situation, notably in housing.[12] The real political challenge for the Kremlin is managing a realistic reform of the defense apparatus, that is, a reform that takes into account the country's socioeconomic conditions.[13] The difficulty thus lies in reconciling the key issue of the military's social condition (a reevaluation of salaries) with a more general rethinking of the allocation of increased financial resources. The defense system has so far been one of the main beneficiaries of this growth, even though it is not yet possible to identify with precision expenses earmarked for equipment, personnel, or exercises.

In addition, the security community's electoral weight must be taken into account: The number of voters with relationships to the security organs—either as military personnel themselves or family members in the services—is estimated to be 7 million (to which 9 million employees of the military-industrial complex and 21 million veterans must be added).[14] As far as the budget is concerned, the real stake lies in the link between the allocation of resources and the progress of reform: Could the High Command improve the pace and range of the reform if it had additional financial resources?[15] Given the lack of transparency in budget information for the military, it is difficult to judge. At the end of Putin's first term, civilian (parliamentary) control over the military budget was presented as a way toward possible reform. According to interviews with members of parliament, however, it seems that no real progress was made in this matter during Putin's second term.[16] The more money the security community gets, it seems, the more secrecy it enjoys.

Security Objectives in the Putin Presidency

Putin has referred to Russian "specificity" on several occasions to justify his political leanings, chosen mode of development, and pace of reform.[17] The "Russian system" translates, among other things, into a deep-rooted rejection of all organizational models imported from abroad.[18] This tendency is probably pushed to the extreme when it comes to politico-military matters, which affect the core of Russia's sovereignty. Advice from abroad in this area in particular is viewed as interference, and even worse, an attempt to purposefully destabilize the Russian security community.

The Russian military's foreign partners would probably benefit from keeping this fear in mind during exchanges so as to prevent misunderstandings. At the same time, the idea is widespread among the Russian elite that the civil-military power distribution is not a problem, insofar as the use of force is not part of Russia's policy tradition.[19] This continued belief that issues of security are not up for debate suggests that the elite faces a problem of political maturity.

At the same time, there is a sort of "securitization" of domestic politics. That happens when "normal politics is pushed into the security realm" and when the political leadership uses "the rhetoric of existential threat" to justify decisions.[20] Obsession with secrecy is one of the most visible signs of "securitization."

Putin is in line with Russian strategic tradition in that, like his predecessors excepting Gorbachev and Yeltsin, his actions have been guided by security objectives. These objectives continue to prevail over other social requirements. The "economy/security dialectic"[21] of his first few years in power gradually became unbalanced, with the security prism distorting the perception and treatment of the majority of presidential concerns, to the detriment of integrating global governance. Thanks to windfall energy revenue in recent years, Putin has managed to increase his options while breaking away from the Yeltsin years.

By making national independence the cornerstone of his policy, Putin has been unable to convince his strategic partners in the West that his intentions are honorable. Indeed by leaving a lingering uncertainty, it is possible for him to favor maneuvers at the expense of objectives.[22] His security and foreign policies subscribe to a historic and strategic Russian tradition that can be summarized as: retain freedom of action, but do nothing with it. In reality, there is an inconsistency in Russian policy that reemerges whenever there is a question of rapprochement in the form of integration. In fact, as soon as any long-term expression of trust in a partner is required, Russia retreats. Part of this attitude can be explained by the framing of the politico-military balance in Russia and the long-standing tradition of suspicion. Massive armed forces and large security services need external and internal threats to justify their importance to the political leadership.

This background is useful to understand Putin's approach to power, which is rooted in an ambivalent political culture. On the one hand, his experience as an intelligence officer working abroad (in the German Democratic Republic in the 1980s) fostered his penchant for compartmentalization, secrecy, and hierarchy. On the other hand, the significance of his political mentor—Anatoly Sobchak, mayor of St. Petersburg during the 1990s—and his initial legal education are not to be underestimated.[23] European in intellectual terms, Putin attaches great importance to the legal aspects of any process. The Kremlin, for example, took the utmost care in destroying the Yukos empire of oil billionaire Mikhail Khodorkovsky through legal decisions. At the risk of being hasty, Putin believes it is politically more natural, simple, and profitable to attack authority in the area of security than on economic grounds or through the treatment of societal problems.

Early in his presidency, Putin faced his first real test in managing a military crisis with the sinking of the nuclear submarine *Kursk* in August 2000. The crisis was symptomatic of the reluctance of the top brass to openly deal with a sensitive problem and to accept foreign help. The military's reluctance to face the facts turned the accident into a catastrophe, not merely for the 118 crew members who perished, but also for the High Command's image. Despite the great emotion manifested in Russia and abroad, Putin avoided tackling the High Command head-on and expressed his intent to bring an end to the poor state of the armed forces—an objective that was compatible with his intent to restore Russian power. One of the most visible consequences of the *Kursk* episode was the decision to increase the military budget at a time when the Russian economy was still very weak.

In retrospect, the *Kursk* incident appears to have been the lowest point of the Russian military's decline. For Putin, the continued acquiescence in the decline of the military was unacceptable, not only because of the consequences for Russia's *prestige* and the credibility of its sea-based nuclear deterrence, but also because of the possible risks posed by a deeply wounded army. This situation could have been used to justify military intervention in domestic politics. In summer 2000, Putin's political base was still very narrow, and a large part of his popularity stemmed from his promise to restore order. That is why Putin exploited the incident to show his attachment to the military.[24]

More deeply, the *Kursk* crisis taught him valuable lessons in communication, making him understand the need to show concern for the victims of such tragedies.[25] The military's imposition of the usual media blackout was simply inappropriate in a modern society with access to various sources of information. In this context, it is better to communicate immediately in order to control the information that is made public than to wait for the military's sanitized explanations. Putin's behavior after the Dubrovka theater incident of 2002, in which Chechen separatists took hostages, and the Beslan school tragedy in 2004 showed that he had learned from the *Kursk* crisis. He was able to use the two subsequent crises to both domestic and external advantage. With Putin, there is a paradox in terms of crisis communication. The Russian security services, and the FSB in particular, were much more involved in the media under Putin than during the Yeltsin period.[26] The security services were active in drafting the legislation preventing media coverage of antiterrorist operations, including the military ones in Chechnya. They are also intrusive and do not hesitate to openly obstruct the investigations by Russian and foreign journalists. However, the traditional media blackout imposed by the military and the security services appears more and more out of date because of society's expectation of information. In the age of the Internet, it is no longer possible to simply be silent. Communication is a key component of Putin's leadership and his relationship with the security community, and he used it as leverage on the security community.

Thanks to Putin, the security community has an improved public image. Yet at the same time, unlimited access to the media is one of Putin's main cards for controlling the security community—through reprimands or praise. His communication advisers encouraged him to develop his image as martial, athletic, and masculine, as opposed to the image of his predecessor, who was much more interested in tennis and drinks. He instantly seized upon military reform as a signature issue, a choice that is undoubtedly explained less by his career as an intelligence officer than by his overarching conception of the state as naturally resting on a strong army.[27] In terms of image, Putin has cleverly exploited the contrast with Yeltsin by preferring to swim laps around the pool rather than relaxing in the sauna.

The development of Putin's communication skills has had an important impact on the perception of his performance in transforming the military. Even highly critical experts believe that his rise to power has marked a turning point in civil control over the military as he managed, in a relatively short amount of time, to reestablish discipline and regain control of the doctrinal production processes. Other experts, however, see no such rupture, as he had been appointed by "the Family" (Yeltsin's entourage) with the tacit agreement of the military. Being initially inexperienced, he did not make his own decisions until his third year in power. With the benefit of hindsight, the second part of 2003 seems to be the pivotal point of Putin's two terms as president. It was then that the Kremlin simultaneously launched an offensive against the

Yukos empire and separated itself from Alexander Voloshin, the Kremlin chief of staff and member of Yeltsin's camp who objected to the moves taken against Khodorkovsky. Again in hindsight, 2003 also appears to be the pinnacle of efforts at internal reform.

Putin's personal influence on the reform movement on the one hand, and on the development of civil-military relations on the other, has given rise to contradictory analyses. For some close to the Kremlin, Putin's control of both the political and military institutions is harmonious, given that no military personality in particular shows credible political ambition. For others, Putin's coming to power has resulted in a degradation of the balance between political and civilian control. Political control would have the most bearing on management, while true civilian control would be broader and would imply a system of checks and balances. If the first were incontestably reinforced, the second would be nipped in the bud.

No Russian analyst regards Putin as having been a pure dictator—he is most often presented as a pragmatic and authoritative politician who used the military as a tool to reinforce his power. His main obstacle was being confronted by a security community that was post-Soviet in structure and partly opposed any idea of reform. His relationship with the security community can be characterized by mixed professional loyalties and differing interests (personal and corporatist in different cases), characteristic of civil-military relations in eighteenth-century European monarchies.[28] This rapprochement provides a clear indication of the direct, unmediated relationship between the president and his armed forces.

Developments in Presidential Statements

Since coming to power, Putin has placed military reform at the top of his agenda. It is one way he has showcased the country's modernization and its capacity to resurrect an ambitious foreign policy, particularly in the post-Soviet universe. His discourse was particularly inflexible after the Beslan hostage incident in 2004. The event's initial shock was reflected in an address he gave on September 4, stating, "We showed weakness. And the weak get beaten." Nine days later, a series of measures were enacted to combat "international terrorism" by reinforcing the unity of the country through a new concentration of power. In a way, these interventions declared a state of war without mentioning—aside from the security services—the full contribution of the security community. Since Beslan, the Kremlin, like the White House since September 11, has considered itself at war against "international terrorism," that is, against any tangible enemy to be fought within a spatial or temporal framework. In his official speeches, Putin has not mentioned reforming the armed forces, concentrating instead on threats and corresponding missions.

Particular developments in his discourse are significant in this respect. In April 2005, his address to the Federal Assembly included a telling omission: the status of the armed forces and military reform.[29] What makes this point worth highlighting is that while Putin has simultaneously stressed the need to establish a democratic and free regime; at no point has he considered the relationship between both civil and military institutions to be a crucial factor in this "democratization." Moreover, he has addressed two issues that are key to that relationship without mentioning the institutions themselves. Putin has presented "international terrorism" as the main threat, but his concern over "reinforcing security" in the southern region has not been followed up by any indication of the role the armed forces might play. As far as Chechnya is concerned, political measures (legislative elections) and economic measures (reconstruction programs) were considered, while the conduct of federal troops and the chain of command were not seen as major obstacles to any attempt at political rule. In the same address, Putin presented the collapse of the USSR as the foremost "geopolitical catastrophe" of the century and emphasized the importance of the commemoration of the sixtieth anniversary of the defeat of Nazi Germany. Both subjects strike a particular chord with the armed forces.

In May 2006, Putin elaborated on security issues in his address to the Federal Assembly. Starting with the terrorist threat and the risks associated with the proliferation of weapons of mass destruction, he emphasized the need to reinforce Russia's nuclear credibility while maintaining traditional forces ready for deployment. He also emphasized the need to avoid repeating the mistakes of the past by allocating too many resources to the armed forces to the detriment of economic development. Addressing the armed forces' operational incapacity at the beginning of his term, Putin presented the results of his policy of increasing military expenditures, reporting that for the first time since 1991 the armed forces were beginning to receive new weapon systems and were increasingly capable of conducting large-scale exercises. According to Putin, the new equipment, exercises, and a favorable climate significantly improved morale among the troops and the officers. Acting as if the structural and operational reforms had been achieved, Putin gave his armed forces the objective—comparable to that of U.S. forces—of being able to intervene, if necessary, simultaneously in conflicts on global, regional, and local fronts.

This development in Putin's discourse raises four hypotheses. The first would be that he has given up developing a new politico-military balance but was satisfied with the balance obtained, which implicitly underlined the undemocratic nature of his regime. (This would be less an affirmation of his own power than a tacit acknowledgment of the difficulty he had in imposing his will to reform on the defense apparatus.) The second would be that he has deemed the issue resolvable through a series of measures, particularly appointments, which remain his main instrument. The third would be that he has dismissed the constitutive value of civil-military power distribution on the entire democratic system and has regarded the controls in place as sufficient. (This hypothesis, however, is contradicted by the time and energy he dedicated to this matter during his first term.) The fourth hypothesis posits that he purposely set unattainable objectives in terms of Russia's economic power precisely so he could continue to exert pressure on the High Command.

Combining the first two hypotheses raises the issue of whether Putin has chosen the status quo in light of the armed forces' inertia, a choice that would account for his policy since 2003. This theory was convincingly advocated by several experts who emphasized that both the Kremlin and the military had an interest in freezing the situation at the beginning of Putin's second term. As to whether Russia needs a strong army, or a massive one, the Kremlin is reluctant to make the choice, according to an expert in nuclear matters. The search for a new status quo can be explained not only by a convergence of interests but also by a lack of strategy on Putin's part. From this point of view, Putin opted to stabilize relations between the civil and military spheres because he simply did not have a detailed plan for reforming the military during his first term. More precisely, because of the nature of his power, he could not get away with directly fighting the High Command.

As in other areas, Putin would have had no real strategy but merely a tactic that favored a flexible stance, which was the main guarantor of his power. With this in mind, the stabilization of civil-military relations can be seen as part of a more general stabilization process rather than one that is transformational. This desire for stabilization surfaced in 2003 with the presidential elections in mind: The clash with Yukos tycoon Mikhail Khodorkovsky alone would suffice as a showcase for reform, national reappropriation, and modernization. Stabilization does not necessarily mean inaction, and certainly Putin used his second term to enforce presidential leadership. For this leadership to be accepted by the military High Command was in itself a change, compared with the military's autonomy during the Yeltsin years. Putin gained respect from the military simply by dealing with military matters "in a serious manner." He essentially understood that "the generals and admirals expected the president to be a leader."[30] The next step was to move from involvement to control.

The notion of control takes on a specific meaning in the civilian-military sphere, as there is a significant difference between Russian and Western experts' idea of "civilian control." For Western experts, the notion goes beyond the decision to use force and directly affects the institutional balance, the definition of political objectives, and the designation of corresponding military targets. Today, as in the past, there would be no sense in talking about "civilian control" of the military in Russia; the term, some experts say, is simply "synonymous with presidential domination."[31]

In any case, the issue has taken a back seat since Putin came to power, according to a general who has been trying for several years to encourage his peers to reflect on the matter. He contends that the main problem consists of differentiating between the subject and the object of control; the difficulty lies in conceiving a global system that integrates political and military power without the domination of one over the other. The subordination of military power to political power, in theory, does not signify that the political sphere evades all forms of control. On the contrary, the political sphere should, according to this general, include itself in the system of controls and integrate the opposition's point of view as well. Such a system would imply relations based on trust. And yet signs, as often voiced in the Russian military press, suggest that trust is in fact waning.[32]

At present, talking about "civilian control" in analyzing the system set up by Putin and his entourage would be a mistake. Real "civilian control" would require a range of checks and balances, as well as the organization and management required for the inspection of the armed forces and the security services. In reality, Putin's disciples set up "administrative control" enabling them to influence all sectors of the country's activity through procedures, regulations, and interventions varying in their directness—and without their having to be answerable. In addition, it is clear that any type of control depends considerably on informal practices between the political leadership and the security community, as well as on personal links among individual actors. That last point is the most difficult to deal with: in any system searching for stability, interpersonal relations are in a constant state of flux.

According to a journalist critical of the Kremlin, it seems clear that "Putin's men," having monopolized power (and wielded it through nominations as well as intimidation), have targeted the security community. According to some analysts, the security community is subjected to both political control (the Kremlin's domination of political life and its instrumentalization of the military in it) and administrative control (living conditions and career management). Administrative control, being the most important, is exercised by the presidential administration through the selection of candidates for the High Command and appointments within the security services. According to an informed observer, this control under Putin was exerted by a "committee" headed by Viktor Ivanov. He was a top aide to the Russian president, who, like Putin, has a KGB/FSB background. It was difficult to get other information on this "committee" through interviews.

Nevertheless, it appears that the presidential administration is not interested in military reform per se but has chosen to focus on the power of nominations, according to a general officer unafraid of drawing a parallel with the Soviet era, casting Viktor Ivanov and Igor Sechin (deputy chief of the presidential administration) in the role of political commissioners. With the ouster of Alexander Voloshin as chief of the presidential administration in October 2003 and of Mikhail Kassianov as prime minister in February 2004, Ivanov and Sechin began using their networks to marginalize other interest groups and to personify de facto the new presidential administration. They also played a key role in the dismantling of Yukos.[33]

This issue of control is delicate to grasp, in that the experts defending the status quo are the very ones who are highlighting the strength of "administrative control." At the same time, they paint the security community as hermetic, rendering all political decisions unpredictable and ineffective. In short, it seems as though administrative control exerts influence primarily through appointments (and, consequently, dismissals). Such an approach is not sufficient for modifying the institutional balance and sense of belonging. In any event, these attempts can only be localized and targeted, at the risk of affecting the *esprit de corps*, which would be a denial, as Samuel Huntington has shown, of the military's unique position.

In reality, to modify behavior within the armed forces, the favored approach has been budgetary—a way that the Kremlin and the government intend to exert tighter and more constant control. However, the transparency of the announced budget far from corresponds to experts' expectations. For 2006, the announcement of the new budget was accompanied by a reclassification of a whole range of accounting information. One Duma delegate noted that although the military budget has been increasing for six years, it is still impossible to precisely quantify where additional resources have been allocated or even the cost of operations in Chechnya.

The lack of budgetary transparency in the security community and the opaque nature of appointments by the Kremlin accentuate the informal aspect of civil-military relations that is prevalent in Russia. More than anywhere else, the play of transversal political-military networks (that is, beyond the hierarchy and extending to the military-industrial complex) fluctuates a great deal, depending on the balance of political power at the time, but especially on the individual economic situation of the players concerned. It undoubtedly has more bearing on their functioning than the principle of the separation of powers in democratic systems (not to mention the weight of the networks in democratic systems, which are clearly more stable). This balance between informal practices and institutional positions is at the core of the relationship. Practical conclusions can be drawn from this fast-moving situation.

First, the debate on the merging of the civil leadership and the military remains crucial. A historical example—the separation of church and state in France in 1905—illustrates the enormous task of "unbundling" the civil and military institutions. Seen this way, the merger represents a certain model of social relations and the base of the political organization; clear separation would entail disorder and a profound reorganization of society.

Second, the status quo thesis, favored by many analysts, is partly relevant. In fact, this thesis gains its full meaning once it is expanded beyond the relationship between the political leadership and the military. Status quo does not necessarily mean inaction, but a way for Putin to strengthen the presidential leadership and to present the Kremlin as the main source of initiatives—the only source of initiatives regarding the military. In other words, the Kremlin's attitude to the military sphere cannot be separated from its attitude toward other spheres, and Putin's personal action with regard to the military cannot be separated from his overall conceptions and practices of reform. As president, Putin was a careful bureaucrat. He remains always attentive to Russian political culture.

Finally, the experts consulted are nearly unanimous in claiming that "civilian control" of Russia's military is nonexistent. However, they have different opinions on the nature of the Kremin's actual control. One thing is certain: During Putin's term, control boiled down to political and administrative control, which enabled the Kremlin to avoid being subjected to any opposition— not from the Duma, not from the expert community, and even less from public opinion. But, at the same time, its action comes up against the security community's lack of transparency.

CHAPTER THREE

Militarization and the *Siloviki*

Accrding to Lilia Shevtsova, there are three components to Putin's power base: big business, liberal-minded technocrats, and federal or regional *apparatchiks* who are put in the same category as *siloviki*.[1] The composition of this group is in fact difficult to clarify. "*Siloviki*" appears to be the key word used by the media and observers to describe Putin's Russia, as "oligarchs" was used to describe Yeltsin's Russia. Vladimir Putin's intelligence officer background is often cited to explain his rise to power, his methods, and his leanings. This focus has gradually been enlarged to include his entourage, a sizable part of which is made up of former security services personnel. However, it remains difficult to really appreciate the *siloviki*'s influence, because the group is probably less an active clan than a media construct, a situation that reflects the prevailing atmosphere in Russia.

"Militarization" and the Ruling Elite

After considerable sociological analysis, Olga Kryshtanovskaya and Stephen White have concluded that Putin's regime was marked by the "militarization" of its elite. Indeed, they took note of the rise to power in presidential, governmental, and regional structures of people with experience in the military, security services, or police.[2] This view has struck a major chord in the media circles and has weighed heavily on foreign perceptions of Putin's regime.

Kryshtanovskaya and White provide figures to illustrate the rise of the *siloviki*'s influence under Putin relative to the Yeltsin era. According to them, Putin has attempted to portray himself as a modernizing Andropov,[3] determined to restore public order and reinforce state power so Russia can regain its international standing. This image was founded in Russian society's call for greater security and stability, while at the same time satisfying the elite's desire for a power organization more in line with its political culture.

Kryshtanovskaya and White believe that Putin's style was based on a network of military and security services personnel, present in all areas, to keep control of all social processes—an approach that is naturally reminiscent of the Soviet era. This well-known argument reinforces the impression of historic permanence that prevails in a large number of analyses that describe the Russian system as being incapable of breaking free of its policing reflexes and condemned to a sort of historic fatalism. It would be tempting to say that "a leopard never changes its spots," given the number of analyses that highlight the *prestige* attached to the services and the military on the one hand, and the tendency to accentuate their future influence on the other hand.[4]

Kryshtanovskaya and White's argument is most interesting in two ways. First, it presents a homogeneous sociology of the elite on which Putin relied, while linking—though not explicitly—the mode of organization and management with Russian political culture. Second, thanks to the *siloviki*, the Russian president was able to use the traditional fusion of civil authority and the military to reinforce his own power and conform to a conception of authority essentially based on control and coercion.

Kryshtanovskaya and White's argument is just as well known in the expert community as it is in the Kremlin. Often discussed, it is used as a reference point in all contemporary assessments of politico-military relations. Adherents view the *siloviki* as a social, corporate, and homogeneous group following a common strategy. Many believe that because of their common culture and origin, the *siloviki* would follow the same path, constituting a sort of party, based on a shared understanding of events and solidarity in a country that does not have any alternative, credible political parties. A second generation of *siloviki* will have thus been formed under Putin. This new generation, unlike that formed under Yeltsin (coming mostly from the military, when numerous generals were elected to the Duma), is seeking economic rather than political influence. According to Brian D. Taylor, the commercialization of the power ministries is "the most fundamental change" in the civilian-military balance since the Soviet collapse.[5] This point is obviously crucial insofar as it explains the confusing entanglement of powers in Russia.

In short, this second generation's main objective is to use state assets for personal gain. Such proclivities come hand in hand with purposely alarmist discourse on the threats Russia currently faces. In reality, under cover of the greater national good (tainted by a whiff of nationalism, and therefore xeno-

phobia and anti-Semitism), personal fortunes are amassed through confisca-
tion, often in a way little different from the Yeltsin era's wild privatizations.[6]
Another feature of this group is its mode of functioning intellectually, characterized by resorting systematically to tactical reasoning, or reducing complex problems to binary logic. In addition, there is a tendency for *siloviki* to
see the world as more organized and coherent than it actually is.

For Kryshtanovskaya, the *siloviki*'s rise to power has resulted in a Soviet-
style organization. In an interview given in 2004, she was even more precise,
highlighting the rise of the "Ivanovs" in spheres of power.[7] This coinage refers
to the key role played in Putin's system by Sergey Ivanov (then minister of
defense) and Viktor Ivanov, not to mention Igor Ivanov, then head of the
Security Council. Kryshtanovskaya also uses the most widespread surname in
Russia to illustrate the current process of social normalization and the standardization of viewpoints. The use of this term also highlights the "Russian-
ness" and the elite's dull homogeneity, fashioned by the security mold as it was
in the Soviet era.

The rise to power of the "Ivanovs" would partly explain the attitudes
prevalent within Russian society. By placing security issues at the heart of his
political action, Putin created a system of power that is firm and stable and
that conforms to the population's expectations. In this, Kryshtanovskaya
contradicts some of her colleagues who conversely believe that Putin's hold
on power could, like the Soviet regime, suddenly collapse. In her opinion,
the *siloviki* draw their strength from their ability to reform or quickly build
new networks of influence, irrespective of the political backdrop. The speed
with which this occurs is clearly enhanced when the Kremlin does not
oppose their influence but instead encourages the establishment of networks from which it may benefit. Kryshtanovskaya regards Russia as being
evidently more democratic and liberal (in economic terms) than it was in
the Soviet era. However, power has now, according to her, entered a phase
of stagnation and will probably not face any major political challenge. Such
stagnation favors the defeat of the opposition, the reinforcement of the
Kremlin's image as the sole center of initiative, and the absence of any real
alternatives.

Several points in Kryshtanovskaya's arguments are worth discussing.
Indeed, going beyond the formal organization of power, they raise the interesting issue of the elite's overall state of mind. This issue is essential to explain
the climate of defiance dominating the heart of Russian society, which functions less like incorporated and connected bodies able to influence presidential policy than transversal networks through which individual and

institutional survival strategies are decided. The *siloviki* share, above all else, common training and reference points that are reflected in their actions.

Yet the divisions between and within the armed forces and the FSB's permanent surveillance of officers should always be borne in mind before attributing too much internal cohesion to the *siloviki*.[8] Putin's main disadvantage stemmed from having attained power without any significant political training or experience. To compensate for that as well as for his lack of imagination, and to try to transform his tactical management into a strategic vision, he surrounded himself with trustworthy men (mainly from St. Petersburg) who shared his way of thinking. Taken as a group, however, "these men [were] barely competent in every area," according to a close observer. They owed their rise to Putin's unexpected ascension; until then, they had, for the most part, "very marginal positions." It is undoubtedly difficult for a foreigner to fully gauge the extent to which "Putin's men" were seen as provincial go-getters among the well-established and traditional leadership. According to a general, Putin's system resembled the rise in power of a "group of Chekists from St. Petersburg" than the rise to power of the *siloviki* as a whole. This reading opens the first gap in Kryshtanovskaya's thesis.

Indeed, Kryshtanovskaya sees members or former members of the KGB/FSB as desiring to take control over the main levers of power.[9] The focus of analysis should, however, be on the nature of individual motivations, given the fact that siloviki can use their positions for personal enrichment: Were they political—aiming to restore Moscow's international influence—or were they rather social—aiming to use membership in the security services as protection? In reality, the main rupture with the Soviet era lies in the significant decrease in the quality of the security services' recruitment.

One journalist who specializes in this issue put it bluntly: "The current level of incompetence and stupidity has never before been reached, even in the Soviet era." The efficiency attributed to Putin at the start of his two terms was gradually eroded and transformed into an inability to carry out reform. This criticism comes in addition to talk of the incompetence of the *siloviki* in administering a country that is simultaneously awaiting structural reform and in the process of rapidly opening up to the world. The *siloviki* worldview and way of functioning make them incapable of grasping the full consequences of the fundamental evolution of Russian society.

Believing themselves to be in control of the entire chain of information, the *siloviki* would thus actually fuel broad disinformation about the regime by focusing the decision-making process on exaggerated threats. This is to the detriment of the country's major challenges, namely, demographic development and attaining a knowledge-based economy with a capacity for innovation. By giving priority to short-term gain—such as the control of energy assets to the Kremlin's benefit—the *siloviki* would in fact be endlessly deferring the long-term decisions the Kremlin needs to make.

Such criticism should not mask an essential fact: In contrast to the Yeltsin period, Russia has regained genuine freedom of action on the international stage. Domestically, even if social disparities have dramatically increased, sustainable economic growth now benefits many parts of society, not only the elite. These are two key arguments for the Kremlin. Analysts close to the Kremlin stress that Russia became both respected and powerful as soon as it stopped copying Western models. This idea is widespread in Russia and to some extent was popularized by the Kremlin itself. Part of the argument is based on the feeling that the United States and European countries tried to pillage Russia during the 1990s.

In this view, the so-called transition was simply a way to force Russia to adopt a behavior that was in accordance with Western standards. According to an analyst close to the Kremlin, in rejecting the principle of Western models on the relationship between civil and military institutions, Putin implicitly rejected any kind of external models. Accordingly, civil-military relations are an essential aspect of Russian specificity and fuel its discourse.

This reading must no doubt be qualified with an additional issue that Western observers tend to mostly ignore: the elite and society's particular relation to time. Today, the profound trauma suffered during the so-called transition period is often forgotten or belittled. It is worth remembering that in Russia an entire generation underwent the switch from a temporal relation that was ideologized and limitless (the construction of socialism) to one that is pragmatic and hectic (individual survival). Western observers think of Russia's development in the medium term (years or decades), whereas Russians, for the most part, continue to map their lives in months or, at most, in semesters. Seen that way, the *siloviki* focus on the control of energy assets is natural politically (use of the country's resources for national purposes), economically (use of price tensions on international energy markets), and in terms of chronological coherence (immediate use within short-term development).

Aside from this temporal link, Putin's entourage shared the same sense of urgency (in terms of seizing a historic and personal opportunity) as well as a "specific mentality," probably struggling to disassociate patriotism and militarism. As a result, in times of crisis, a scapegoat was sought (Beslan and Ukraine were significant in this respect). This entourage upheld the idea of a Russia that was fundamentally threatened, and thus tended to conceive mobilization or national impetus only in terms of security or the reinforcement of Russian power.

This is notably found in the economic arena, where Putin's administration sought to establish large companies—national champions capable of playing an active role in global markets. However, the administration quickly became nervous with regard to the prospect of an emerging civil society that would be less dependent on the state. Finally, Putin's entourage regarded the pyramid structure of the military as the ultimate model of efficiency. According to a journalist who specializes in defense matters, such a structure "preserves a model inherited from the nineteenth century, whereby the ministers are accountable to the prime minister and directly to the president/czar for all security-related issues."

Yet the real difficulty with this type of approach lies in delineating Putin's team associations with precision, particularly with regard to civil-military matters, where the inherent secrecy makes it difficult to identify a permanent team. What is more, it is not even clear that there is such a "permanent team." Indeed, Putin's entourage seems to be perpetually in flux, contingent on the situation and issues at hand.

Putin's Circles

The heart of the civil-military power distribution therefore lies in Putin's circle of advisers and the link between the sociological composition of Putin's circle and his own presidential leanings. There is nothing obvious about this link. Indeed, backgrounds and professional careers are not themselves sufficient for predicting political choices. However, Kryshtanovskaya and White determined that the *siloviki* are sufficiently homogeneous to guide public politics, and they cite as examples the *siloviki*'s influence on patriotic education in schools, the offensive against foreign nongovernmental organizations, the reinforcement of the state in controlling energy resources, and the increase in the budget for the armed forces. Kryshtanovskaya and White further their analysis by concentrating on Putin's informal social circles.[10]

According to this analysis, and despite the evident difficulty in qualifying or quantifying the *siloviki*, the ruling Russian elite as of January 2005 totaled 1,057 people, broken down as follows: 24 members of the Security Council; 36 members of the presidential administration; 72 members of government; 178 members of the Federation Council; 450 deputies to the Duma; 88 regional governors; 120 members of the affairs committee; seven official envoys; and 82 federal inspectors. Having conducted a number of interviews with people both in and near this group, Kryshtanovskaya and White concluded that beyond the three main official structures (the government, the Security Council, and the presidential administration), three teams revolved around Putin. The prime minister, purportedly responsible for the country's social and economic policies, has authority over neither power ministries nor security services. In theory, the Security Council ensures the coordination of the different security bodies. However, since it was founded, it has never been able to establish itself as the principal mechanism in the political-military chain, capable of synthesizing positions and overseeing the execution of decisions.

This is the result of Yeltsin's chosen mode of government, which had encouraged rivalry among the ministries, and of the political weakness of successive secretaries of the Security Council—Putin being the notable exception. Putin deftly used his Security Council role and his position as former head of the FSB in his steady rise to power in the Kremlin. His Security Council role, which he assumed in March 1999, was the last position he held prior to being named prime minister by Yeltsin in August 1999. Earlier, he was deputy chief of presidential staff (August 1996); first deputy chief of presidential staff (May 1998); and director of the FSB (July 1998). The Security Council and FSB positions served as preparation for handling the second war in Chechnya, which occurred shortly after Putin's appointment as prime minister in 1999. He was thus able to gain the appreciation of the military while at the same time pledging loyalty to the "Yeltsin family."

Table 3-1 shows the three main official structures revolving around Putin as of January 2008. The most striking aspect in terms of power distribution is that a person can be a government minister and simultaneously be active in a company.

Beyond their official portfolios, table 3-2 lists two groups that met at the Kremlin on Mondays and Saturdays to make strategic decisions under Putin. The Monday meetings often received greater media coverage than the Saturday meetings (they were in part broadcast on television). A third, unofficial team of Putin's personal friends met informally at Putin's residence. The frequency, composition, and object of these meetings are shrouded in mystery.

Two men—Dmitry Medvedev and Sergey Ivanov—were members of all three groups and were also members of the government and the Security Council. It is worth noting that until December 2007, both men, who were very close to Putin, were considered to be rivals for the Russian presidency. On the surface, this opposition was maintained by the Kremlin to give the impression of two different paths for Russia's development. Both were of the same hierarchical level, namely, first deputy prime minister. Medvedev was promoted as a loyal fellow from St. Petersburg with a technocrat background and was reputed to be more interested in a partnership with the West, while Ivanov, who also hailed from Leningrad, was described as Putin's double from the security services and was seen as the candidate of the *siloviki.* In reality, things are far more complicated than they seem. First and foremost, the difference in their profiles is striking.

Sergey Ivanov was born in 1953. Prior to becoming first deputy prime minister in February 2007, he was deputy prime minister (November 2005), a role that he combined with his position as minister of defense (March 2001). He was also responsible for the military-industrial complex and military cooperation with other countries. A graduate in modern languages from Leningrad State University (1975), he enrolled in advanced KGB training until 1981. Expelled from Great Britain in 1983 under suspicion of espionage, his entire career was spent with the security services (KGB, SVR, and FSB, with prolonged stays in Finland and Kenya), before serving as secretary of the Security Council from November 1999 to March 2001 (he remains a permanent member of the Security Council). Like Putin, he reached a very high level in the security services.

Dmitry Medvedev was born in 1965. Before becoming first deputy prime minister in November 2005, he was chairman of the board at Gazprom and a permanent member of the Security Council. A law graduate from St. Petersburg State University (1990), he met Putin at the Committee for External Relations in St. Petersburg and followed him to Moscow. He headed Putin's presidential campaign in 2000, then took on responsibilities within the presidential administration as Alexander Voloshin's "right hand" and with Gazprom before becoming chief of the presidential staff, a position he held from October 2003 to November 2005. As first deputy prime minister, he was in charge of the so-called national projects that the Kremlin wanted to implement (demography, health care, education, housing, and agriculture). On December 10, 2007, he was appointed by Putin and four parties including *Yedinaya Rossiya* as their common candidate for the presidential elections in March 2008. The next day, Dmitry Medvedev asked Putin to become his prime minister. He became president on May 7, 2008.

Two other key figures must be mentioned with regard to the politico-military establishment and the Kremlin, even though they acted backstage rather than in the limelight. Both Viktor Ivanov and Igor Sechin are important figures in the system and had direct access to Putin.

Viktor Ivanov was born in 1950 in Novgorod. He became a personal adviser to the Russian president in March 2004, responsible for personnel, the

Table 3-1. Main Institutions in January 2008

Government	Security Council	Presidential Administration
Viktor Zubkov, prime minister	Vladimir Putin, president of the Russian Federation	Sergey Sobyanin, chief of staff of the Presidential Executive Office; head of the supervisory board at TVEL (a consortium for the production and commercialization of nuclear fuel)
Sergey Ivanov, first deputy prime minister		
Dmitry Medvedev, first deputy prime minister; chairman of Gazprom's board of directors	*Permanent members*	
	Boris Gryzlov, chairman of the State Duma	
	Viktor Zubkov, prime minister	
Alexander Zhukov, deputy prime minister; chairman of the board of directors of RGD (Rossijskie zheleznye dorogi, the Russian railway)	Sergey Ivanov, first deputy prime minister	Vladislav Surkov, deputy chief (interior and federal policy), of the Presidential Executive Office; aide to the president; member of the management board at Transnefteprodukt
	Sergey Lavrov, minister of foreign affairs	
	Dmitry Medvedev, first deputy prime minister; chairman of Gazprom's board of directors	
Alexey Kudrin, deputy prime minister/minister of finance; member of Sberbank's management board	Sergey Mironov, head of the Federation Council	Igor Sechin, deputy chief (general affairs) of staff of the Presidential Executive Office; aide to the president; head of Rosneft's management board
	Rashid Nurgaliev, minister of the interior	
Sergey Naryshkin, deputy prime minister/head of the governmental administration; member of Rosneft's management board	Nikolay Patrushev, director of the FSB	
	Anatoly Serdyukov, minister of defense	
	Sergey Sobyanin, head of the presidential administration	*Advisers*
Tatiana Golikova, minister of health and social development		Alexander Abramov (relations with the parliament and presidential domestic trips)
	Mikhail Fradkov, head of the SVR	
Alexey Gordeyev, minister of agriculture		Alexander Beglov (legislative activities)
Dmitry Kozak, minister of regional development	*Council members*	Larisa Brycheva (justice)
	Yury Baluyevsky, chief of the General Staff	Viktor Ivanov (management); head of the management boards at Aeroflot and Almaz-Antei
Sergey Lavrov, minister of foreign affairs	Anatoly Kvashnin, presidential envoy	
Igor Levitin, minister of transport; member of the management board at RGD	Ilya Klebanov, presidential envoy	
		Dzhakhan Pollyeva (education and science)
	Alexander Konovalov, presidential envoy	Sergey Prikhodko (international relations); member of the management board at Sukhoi
Elvira Nabiullina, minister of economic development and commerce; member of the management boards at Sberbank, Gazprom, and RAO UES	Alexey Kudrin, deputy prime minister/minister of finance; member of Sberbank's management board	
		Igor Shuvalov (national projects and G8 sherpa); member of RGD's management board
	Pyotr Latyshev, presidential envoy	

Table 3-1 (continued) Main Institutions in January 2008

Government	Security Council	Presidential Administration
Rashid Nurgaliev, minister of the interior	Yury Ossipov, head of the Academy of Science	Sergey Yastrzhembsky (relations with the European Union)
Vladislav Putilin, deputy chairman with ministerial status of the Military-Industrial Commission	Georgy Poltavchenko, presidential envoy	
	Grigory Rapota, presidential envoy	*Presidential Plenipotentiary Envoys to the Federal Districts*
Leonid Reyman, minister of information technology and communication	Vladimir Ustinov, minister of justice	Anatoly Kvashnin
	Yury Chaika, prosecutor general	Georgy Poltavchenko
		Ilya Klebanov
Anatoly Serdyukov, minister of defense	Sergey Shoigu, minister for emergency situations	Pyotr Latyshev
		Alexander Konovalov
Alexander Sokolov, minister of culture and communication		Grigory Rapota
		Oleg Safonov
Yury Trutnev, minister of natural resources		*Aides*
		Aslambek Aslakhanov (North Caucasus)
Vladimir Ustinov, minister of justice		Yury Laptev (culture)
Andrey Fursenko, minister of education and science		Mikhail Lesin (media, information, intellectual property)
Viktor Khristenko, minister of industry and energy; chairman of Transneft's management board; member of the management boards at Gazprom, RGD, and RAO UES (electricity monopoly)		Anatoly Pristavkin (amnesty)
		Sergey Samoilov (federalism and local self-administration)
		Gennady Troshev (Cossacks)
		Sergey Ushakov (adviser)
		Vladimir Shevchenko (adviser)
Sergey Shoigu, minister for emergency situations		Veniamin Yakovlev (justice)
		Representatives
		Alexander Kotenkov (Federation Council)
		Alexander Kosopkin (Duma)
		Mikhail Krotov (institutional court)
		Alexey Gromov, press attaché for the president
		Igor Schegolev, chief of the presidential protocol

Sources : <www.government.ru>, <www.scrf.gov.ru>, <www.kremlin.ru>.

Table 3-2. Table 3-2: Putin's Informal Social Circles (2004–2006)

Team 1—Monday	Team 2—Saturday	Team 3—Informal
Mikhail Fradkov, prime minister	Mikhail Fradkov, prime minister	Sergey Ivanov, minister of defense, deputy prime minister
Alexander Jukov, deputy prime minister	Sergey Ivanov, deputy prime minister	Igor Sechin, deputy chief of presidential staff; head of Rosneft's management board
German Gref, minister of economic development and commerce; member of the management boards at Sberbank, Gazprom, and RAO UES	Dmitry Medvedev, first deputy prime minister; chairman of Gazprom's board of directors	Dmitry Medvedev, first deputy prime minister; chairman of Gazprom's board of directors
Mikhail Zurabov, minister of social affairs	Sergey Lavrov, minister of foreign affairs	Viktor Cherkesov, head of the federal service for the control of narcotics
Sergey Naryshkin, head of the governmental administration	Igor Ivanov, secretary of the Security Council	Dmitry Kozak, presidential envoy to the Caucasus
Igor Sechin, deputy chief of presidential staff; head of Rosneft's management board	Nikolay Patroushev, director of the FSB	Vladimir Kozhin, adviser to the president
Dmitry Medvedev, first deputy prime minister; chairman of Gazprom's board of directors	Rashid Nourgaliev, minister of the interior	German Gref, minister of economic development and commerce; member of the management boards at Sberbank, Gazprom, and RAO UES
Sergey Ivanov, minister of defense, first deputy prime minister	Sergey Lebedev, head of the SVR	Georgy Poltavchenko, presidential envoy
Sergey Lavrov, minister of foreign affairs	*Occasional participants*	
Rashid Nurgaliev, minister of the interior	Viktor Ivanov, adviser to the president; head of Aeroflot's management board	
Occasional participants	Igor Sechin, deputy chief of presidential staff; head of Rosneft's management board	
Alexey Gordeyev, minister of agriculture	Vladimir Ustinov, former prosecutor general and minister of justice	
Yury Trutnev, minister of natural resources		
Igor Levitin, minister of transport		
Sergey Yastrzhembsky, adviser for relations with the European Union		

Adapted from Olga Kryshtanovskaya and Stephen White, "Inside the Putin Court: A Research Note," *Europe-Asia Studies*, vol. 57, no. 7.

public sector, constitutional rights, the nomination of judges, pardons, and awards. At the same time, he is head of the management boards at Aeroflot and the Almaz-Antei consortium, which consists of 46 companies and is known for the production and commercialization of the S-300 surface-to-air missile. He graduated from the Institute for Electrotechnology in Leningrad (1974) and underwent advanced training with the KGB in 1978. He rose through the ranks of the KGB in Leningrad and served in Afghanistan (1987–1988) before heading the mayor's administration in St. Petersburg (1994–1998). Appointed to Moscow, he headed the FSB's department for economic security before joining the presidential staff.

Igor Sechin was born in 1960 in Leningrad. He became deputy chief of the presidential staff in 2000 and, since July 2004, simultaneously served as head of the management board at Rosneft. He holds a degree in Portuguese from Leningrad State University and served in Angola and Mozambique as a military interpreter from 1984 to 1986. On returning to Leningrad, he held different administrative posts before becoming head of the committee for external relations. He joined the presidential staff in 1996 and the chief of the presidential administration's secretariat in 1998 before becoming deputy chief of the secretariat in 2000.

The Role and Myth of the FSB

Any analysis of Putin's inner circle comes up against methodological issues surrounding the natural, if debatable, tendency toward "institutionalization," that is, to assume that such institutions as the Ministry of Defense or FSB standardize the behavior of the people associated with them. Depending on the perspective, it leads to incomplete analyses, presenting the FSB, the General Staff, or the army as coherent players. These shortcuts prevail in both the analyses of Putin's regime and in the discourse of our interlocutors, resulting quite often in a black-and-white representation of power relations. Such a representation is often incorrect, but it is nevertheless useful, because almost all analysts and people questioned base their reasoning on Putin's system—and therefore their reaction to it—by coming back to this sort of simplification.

By affirming, for example, that "civilian control is political control exercised by the FSB," a journalist scrutinizing Kremlin life raises more questions than he answers. [11] Such a statement amounts to a claim that, on the one hand, the army is subordinated to the FSB, and that, on the other hand, Putin, having come from the FSB, used his prior service to manage the civil-military power distribution.

It must be noted that there is some confusion over "militarization" and "FSB-ization." Some use these terms interchangeably to highlight the influence of the *siloviki* over the Kremlin and Russian society. "Militarization" would thus in fact be the work of the security services and, in particular, the FSB. The aim would not so much be to appoint military personnel to positions of responsibility, but to propagate a discourse founded on security issues across the wide spectrum of society, including the leading elite, to maintain a state of "prewar"—justifying exceptional measures and reinforcing its overall weight on the whole system.

From this perspective, the military is less an FSB target than is society— leading some experts to present Viktor Ivanov as a regime ideologist. Ivanov coordinated the Kremlin message while appointing loyal men to state offices and beyond (especially in companies deemed to be of strategic interest). Those surrounding him led wide-ranging offensives, from carving up Yukos to manipulating elections and military reform, designed to gain the greatest control in the least amount of time. This reading diminishes the central role of state-military relations, turning the military into just another theater of Kremlin control operations.

A crucial finding emerged during this research. Indeed, not a single person interviewed for the book was able to list the members of the group surrounding Viktor Ivanov, thereby reinforcing the overall impression of mystery. Such a fog gives rise to three theories. First, that there has been a seizure of power by the Vladimir Putin–Viktor Ivanov–Sergey Ivanov triumvirate, the functioning of which remains enigmatic and is limited to former FSB agents, keeping the military *sensu stricto* at a distance. Alternatively, it is argued that the Kremlin is attempting to mystify its power, a theory that is propagated more or less consciously by Russian experts in deference to their Western colleagues, in order to illustrate their arguments on the consequences of super-presidentialism for Russia. The third thesis is that the capacity of the FSB and the security services to act was overestimated by the Russian expert community and, consequently, its Western counterpart. Such an overestimation may be explained by a backward-looking fascination with the KGB's power in Soviet society or by giving undue credit to actors because their motives and actions are too difficult to decrypt or explain.

There is, to quote one expert on security policies in Russia, a "persistent myth" surrounding the KGB/FSB both in Russia and abroad. This myth explains service members' professionalism and duty to the state. Yet the notion of the public good would have been supplanted, due to the radical socioeconomic changes of the last decade, by self-interest and desire for personal gain.

As far as the presumed professionalism is concerned, recruitment for both organizations has declined. Because of low wages, it was difficult for the armed forces and the security services to attract recruits during the 1990s unless they tolerated, suggested, or even encouraged supplemental income.

However, general references to military wages are misleading because they do not account for the complex nature of the Russian service.[12] In January 2007, for instance, just after having been commissioned, a junior lieutenant officially earned 830 rubles ($34 in 2007) per month. But he would get 2,250 rubles ($92 in 2007) for being a platoon commander. Added to this are various bonuses for location, specific units, academic qualifications, and types of service. As a result, pay for servicemen within the armed forces and the security services varies widely. This fact should be borne in mind when one mentions the homogeneity, in this case financial, of the *siloviki.*

Within the *siloviki,* the security services—especially the FSB—are usually seen as the core. It is often said that under Putin these institutions widely influenced the elite as well as the society. Yet it is no longer possible to ascribe to them the same structural character as in the Soviet era. The opening up of the Russian system to the "global market" has meant that far more attractive jobs (in terms of salary, responsibility, and international contacts) outside of the services have been created.

Herein lies one of the most fundamental breaks with the past: By losing their monopoly over the international opportunities, the security services have become less attractive in the eyes of the next generation. The phenomenon is clearly magnified for the armed forces, which—besides their loss of social status owing both to extremely precarious living conditions and the downward spiral of operations during the 1990s—have struggled to offer attractive career options for young people. The importance of the security services and the armed forces therefore looks set to decline over the coming years if military salaries remain unchanged, as these groups become increasingly ill-adapted to economic growth that is opening up career opportunities and enabling the emergence of the middle class beyond the reach of the military.

Nevertheless, the arguments put forward by Olga Kryshtanovskaya and Stephen White influence a number of interpretations of Putin's Russia. Their use of the term "militarization" reinforces the traditional understanding of a merger between the civilian and military elite by maintaining a confusion of sorts between the military and the security services. On the one hand, this association is undoubtedly pertinent in terms of promoting a philosophy in which security—both domestic and external—is the primary objective of the ruling elite. On the other hand, these theories fail to highlight the strong tensions existing among the *siloviki*, as their main objective is likely to be financial rather than security.

As a consequence, the civil-military center of gravity is noticeably displaced. The conceptually based balance between civilian power and military power in Russia is complicated by the security services. The services' *prestige* among the ruling elite is indisputable. However, to appreciate the true balance of power, it is not enough to simply attribute this to Putin's history with the security services. Here, as elsewhere, individual and institutional positions fluctuate enormously, rendering more difficult any attempt at schematization. Putin has built his popularity on an image of pragmatism and efficiency. Without any true political experience, he established himself through technical and managerial measures. With that in mind, it was essential for Putin that Russia be perceived both at home and abroad as a state capable of raising taxes, imposing regional decisions, and limiting the ambitions of the oligarchs.

Today an ambivalent image of political communication is prevalent among members of the expert community. Russia appears to be an inefficient state with only virtual power, unable to cope with real challenges. At the same time, Russia has undoubtedly had many successes, for instance in foreign policy. These successes since 2000 are a stark contrast with the reality of a group of mostly incompetent and unscrupulous leaders who seek quick gains in foreign policy rather than rebuilding, both conceptually and operationally, a true defense system.[13]

Kryshtanovskaya's argument has been subject to criticism that deserves elaboration.[14] She sanctions the concept of an all-powerful *siloviki*, when in fact this group is far more complex. Strong internal rivalries and circumstantial alliances exist within the *siloviki*. Unlike with the oligarchs, being specific about them is far more difficult, since they hold various levels of responsibility in Moscow and in the regions. Of course, the mention of their rise to power refers to an active minority integrated into the decision-making mechanisms and inner political circles. Taken as a whole, the *siloviki* primarily exist as a result of the atmosphere of control that they help maintain in society.

"FSB-ization" Versus "Militarization"

The term "militarization" has been widely used to describe the evolution of Putin's regime. This is, in fact, a misconception: Of all the security services, it was the military with which Putin feels most ill at ease.[15] In retrospect, it is interesting to read the comments made in the press shortly after he came to power. At the time, Putin was said to be trying hard to immediately reduce the influence of the military and prevent opposition.[16] To do so, and because of the narrowness of his early political base, Putin drew from the security services the managers necessary to consolidate his power.[17]

In hindsight, it appears that the military initially viewed Putin as a credible leader because of his background in the intelligence community. From the beginning, Putin used the similarities between the military and the services to his advantage, in particular the bureaucratic hierarchical structure.[18] In addition, on many occasions, he used the high morale of the FSB as an example for the military to emulate.[19]

Given this background, many security experts do not feel comfortable with the notion of militarization. Rather, they prefer the use of "FSB-ization" or "policization," and even of "special force-ization." The fight against "international terrorism" subsequently provided a pretext to justify the coordination of different state structures and to open a politico-operational space favorable to the security services. In addition, the fight against terrorism has given the FSB supplementary funds and enabled it to regain control of customs and parts of FAPSI. Since the reforms implemented in March 2003, the FSB is clearly the leading service within the security community. The general perception of "FSB-ization" under Putin corresponds mainly to the strengthening of the FSB as an institution. From this point of view, the 2003 reforms have dramatically affected the civil-military balance. Since then, part of Putin's problem has been determining how to bring the FSB under tight presidential control.[20]

In fact, the FSB has managed, through the extension and renewal of its networks, to exert its influence beyond defending corporatist interests by contributing to the control of the military's High Command.[21] It now has a direct influence on Russia's strategic agenda.[22] This extension of influence is due to the trust Putin placed in the FSB at the beginning of his first term as president. He did so at the risk of rendering himself dependent upon the FSB later, thereby making the issue of democratic control of the intelligence services more relevant than ever.[23]

Moreover, the FSB's increase in influence may ultimately prove to be counterproductive in terms of economic modernization and industrial restructuring. Despite its self-confidence, the FSB is scarcely prepared to manage all the industrial complexes with international standing. This last point is crucial, as it implies that the FSB is hampering the Kremlin's efforts at economic modernization through national champions. This is less a conscious desire to block these efforts than a profound inability to accept the inevitable consequences of a market economy (not in terms of personal gain but in terms of the entrepreneurial spirit, risk taking, and opening up to the world). The services have a greater interest in perpetuating defiance than in conveying self-confidence. In this spirit, they conceive of economic activity as they do their own political action: surveillance, control, and manipulation. In many cases, the *siloviki* affililiated with large companies go to great lengths to explain that their mission is to fix the problems the oligarchs created and to restore order to develop Russian business.[24] In practice, however, they appear to use their positions within the state apparatus to promote their personal and financial interests.[25] As Putin's double term comes to an end, the Russian elite is certainly "more bourgeois than militocratic."[26]

Some experts close to the Kremlin believe that the services' attitude reflects the population's expectations. During the Yeltsin years, the public, desiring order and stability, trusted the military personnel involved in politics as representing three values: "dignity, honesty, and discipline." Under Putin, this expectation with regard to the military has shifted toward the security services, whose members are considered by the population to be "intellectual, modern, and patriotic" and embodying a "modernized patriotism." Today, the contrast between the image of an aging, archaic army and that of young, entrepreneurial services is very strong. This is the image promoted by some of the Kremlin's public relations officers, particularly vis-à-vis their foreign contacts. The members of *Yedinaya Rossiya* have no doubt that Putin was aiming to reinforce his hold over administrative processes through an inner circle that is "more aware of organization and efficiency than militarization."

Experts close to the Yabloko party or SPS (a union of right-wing forces that forms the liberal camp with Yabloko) are far more alarmist in their judgment of the regime's evolution, highlighting the ravages that racketeering has inflicted within the services. According to these individuals, the security community has never been so divided, as many of its members attempt to use their position to develop their own enterprises. Their efforts to reap profit from their position according to the place in the hierarchy revive social rivalries to the detriment of solidarity. The army does not seem capable of thwarting the services' rise to power, which relies on very powerful industrial groups headed by Gazprom and Rosneft. Meanwhile, elite units such as the Alpha group can no longer bear to see their colleagues help themselves become richer and turn into the new oligarchs, according to one member of Yabloko.

The most frequent criticism made of Kryshtanovskaya's argument rests in recalling the silent rivalry between the armed forces and the intelligence services responsible for their monitoring. To this basic duality can be added strong internal tensions within both the military and the services. The rivalry between the armed forces and the KGB/FSB is a historic one. In the Soviet era, central authorities deliberately stoked it to reduce the influence of each and avoid dependency. The rivalry is also explained by their contradictory missions. While the military profession is based on perpetual silence over state affairs and apolitical conduct, the services are responsible for monitoring activities within the state and society—an eminently political task. In other words, the army avoids the political arena, while the services control it.

This fundamental opposition voids the notion of "militarization" as a political mode of organization. Moreover, "militarization" is associated with the idea of conspiracy—a historically widespread perception of Russian (and Soviet) power both within Russia and abroad. In this context, such a conspiracy theory would mean that, acting secretly, the small group of *siloviki* is following Putin's orders to sustain a strategy dedicated to restoring Russian power.

This argument is rebuffed by those who believe that Putin's associates, despite having spent the first part of their careers with the KGB/FSB, have been limited by the realities of Moscow and the functioning of the administration on a federal scale. This thinking holds that by following certain professional trajectories while maintaining their own approaches (which combines a superiority complex from the services and an inferiority complex from the provinces—many of them came from St. Petersburg), they have also been completely transformed by their experience in power and their astounding social rise.

The change in the level of their responsibilities has forced them to adapt, meaning that the Putin-controlled conspiracy theory is difficult to uphold. The conspiracy theory is, however, still used to describe the presidential administration's mode of functioning—a "black box" that purposely ignores external advice and makes decisions cut off from society. By being able to resort to coercion only in isolated, exemplary cases—unlike its Soviet predecessors, who had the luxury of resorting to coercion at any time—the presidential administration often gives the impression of being disconnected from social realities.

Concerning the military, the rejection of the conspiracy theory entails a questioning of the existence of an organized military lobby capable of defining and defending its interests. In reality, it seems fairer to talk of fragmented lobbies (especially in the nuclear and aeronautic fields). Some analysts also stress these groups' capacity to influence policy and opinion through their links to the parliament, the regional elite, and the media. However, these groups did not resist the Kremlin's attempts to reorganize the military-industrial complex in a way comparable to the reorganization of the energy sector. Naturally, this is a process that could have an indirect effect on the relationship between the armed forces and the military-industrial complex.

In the same way, the progressive "FSB-ization" of the decision-making processes did not begin with Putin. An analysis of appointments shows that Putin has followed a trend largely begun by his predecessor, who had "a *silovik* problem."[27] In the fine tradition of merging the civilian and military realms, Putin found power structures already infiltrated by the military and the security services; his capacity to renew management was, in reality, limited. The "mini-purges" he resorted to were when his power was at its highest point.

Other analysts see a fundamental difference between members of the military and the security services, considering service members to be capable of more coordinated influence than those in the military. Even if it is difficult to tell who pursued daily military reform within the presidential administration, it appears that the Kremlin exercised control over the military via the security services, which heightened animosity between the two spheres, according to a journalist who specializes in the subject. This dualism is strongly qualified by analysts who left the army during the 1990s and stress that the original corps affiliation matters far less than the position occupied, the sphere of activities, and the access to financial means.

Regarding state-military relations, the mere terms "militarization" and "*siloviki*" are misleading and distort the analysis of Putin's regime. It is clear that power has shifted from the security services to the president. Yet that alone cannot explain the functioning of a regime that is far more disorganized and unpredictable than its hierarchical and structured appearance make it seem. In this respect, "militarization" is a misleading term—giving the impression that the overrepresentation of the *siloviki* among the ruling elite has repercussions for the whole of society. This overrepresentation stems from the predominance of security issues over other issues such as social development. And while this is in keeping with Russia's tradition of authority, the population's indoctrination is not comparable to that of the Soviet era.

Ultimately the very notion of *siloviki* is vague. Indeed, as previously noted, while it recalls an organized and structured group, it is striking to note the extent to which heterogeneity prevails in reality, as observed in interviews with Russians and through examining Russian political life. What is more, internal rivalry is poorly measured because it opposes fluctuating networks rather than firmly constituted corps: Original corps affiliation matters far less than the position occupied at the time of analysis.

This last observation is particularly important with regard to relations between military and security service members within various fields of activity, such as the military-industrial complex or the energy sector. Indeed, it is particularly in this type of sector that personal power is exerted—more so, in fact, than having good relations with the Kremlin. The real issue at stake has been the capacity of the military and service members to assume "managerial" functions within global industrial groups. The primary tension lies precisely in the contradiction between Putin's quest to modernize the economy by relying on service members and their own weak entrepreneurial culture, which favors a logic of corruption. Conversely, an entrepreneur who does not come from the intelligence service, or is beyond a certain level of development or notoriety, is clearly at risk of being controlled by members of the security service.

Sergey Ivanov's Document: Change Without Change

In May 1997, Yeltsin appointed Igor Sergeyev as minister of defense. Four years later, and one year after Putin's first election, the appointment of Sergey Ivanov marked a turning point in the development of civil-military relations in Russia. It has been portrayed as a realignment in favor of political power, having managed to impose a "civilian" at the head of the Ministry of Defense—a step forward compared to Andrey Kokoshin's experience. As deputy minister of defense, Kokoshin came up against the weight of the military-industrial complex, which desired to shield itself from all external scrutiny. Despite his expertise in the field, he never managed to achieve acceptance of the notion of civilian control over a military institution.

Sergey Ivanov left his post in February 2007. Some experts believe that he succeeded in becoming the most powerful minister of defense since Dmitry Ustinov, who served from 1976 to 1984.[28] Before his appointment, Ivanov had led the Security Council, and before that he climbed all the echelons of the intelligence officer ladder, including assignments abroad. Yet Sergey Ivanov is considered a civilian "because he is not military," as a retired general put it. His personality and experiences of his first year in office, which saw a rapprochement with the United States after the 9/11 terrorist attacks, generated great tension between the Kremlin and the High Command because of his clear ambitions to reestablish the predominance of the High Command. It is worth remembering that Yeltsin made the General Staff and the Ministry of Defense parallel organizations equally subordinated to the president. Sergey Ivanov had to deal with a High Command that was still marked by rivalry between Igor Sergeyev and Anatoly Kvashnin, the head of the General Staff, who openly ignored his minister. Kvashnin seemingly was at the height of his power at the time.[29]

The appointment of Sergey Ivanov can be understood in one of three ways: as a desire to rebalance the civil and military spheres; as a message to the military regarding the need for reform; or as an extension of the security services' zone of action.

The first view is the least convincing, insofar as an appointment, even at this high level, is not enough to modify institutional structure. It is certainly an important step, but one that could become significant only in conjunction with a mass influx of competent civilians in the Ministry of Defense—a shift that was not really encouraged. (Such a twofold movement was, however, implemented in the former member countries of the Warsaw Pact.)[30]

The second view is more convincing: that the military has a tendency to reduce reform to technical provisions resulting in new allocations of resources. Ivanov's appointment reminded the military that no real reform would be possible without recasting the whole of civil-military relations.

The third view—that Putin exercised political control over the generals via Sergey Ivanov—is the most realistic.[31] "It is he who guarantees the army's loyalty in Putin's eyes, simply by playing the role of the Kremlin's political commissioner," according to an analyst. A journalist adds: "Sergey Ivanov only controls the loyalty of the army and is completely uninterested in military reform."

Several sources stress the close and personal relationship between Putin and Sergey Ivanov. The problem the Russian president faced in March 2001 was not to choose between a military man, a civilian, or a "disguised civilian," but to find a trustworthy man. The key element for the politico-military relationship lies in the existence of the Putin–Ivanov duo, within which it is not always easy to distinguish who was the driving force. Touted as a likely presidential successor to Putin until December 2007, Sergey Ivanov has been the subject of various analyses focusing on his political experience. Some had long warned that, lacking "vision or political support," he was far from a certain bet. Others, by contrast, thought he was of "true political caliber." He was chosen as minister of defense not because of his career in the intelligence services, but because of his ability to neutralize the High Command opposition to Putin. His professional background also would have been less of a decisive factor in his appointment than his friendship with Putin. But perhaps this friendship would not have been as strong without shared professional and geographical origins.

In the chess match between the High Command and the Kremlin, Sergey Ivanov embodied the Kremlin's "major piece." Nevertheless, he often found it difficult to establish himself with the military institution and, consequently, was often called on to resign. Step by step, however, he succeeded in consolidating his personal power by establishing strong links with the military-industrial complex, one of his favorite tools for influencing the military.

The peculiarity of the civil-military system was the lack of interface between the presidential administration and the Ministry of Defense. To gain support, Sergey Ivanov appointed a number of service members (from the FSB, SVR, and FSO) to the defense apparatus.[32] The relationship between the "civilian" services and the GRU (which depends upon the General Staff) has traditionally been characterized by rivalry, stoked by the services personnel's command and logistical incompetence.[33] Despite his attempts to circumvent the military institution's key bodies, Sergey Ivanov immediately came up against the generals' opaque corporatism. Taken as a whole, their attitude remains hostile toward democratization within the military. From the generals' perspective, democratic development would inevitably result in a decline of their privileges, such as being able to use conscripts as they please.

Aside from official appointments, Sergey Ivanov tried to establish himself by attempting to take control of doctrinal production. Some experts believe that this was partly to please Western partners, as it would have been the surest way of giving the impression of change without actually changing anything. Essentially, Igor Ivanov, in coordination with Vladimir Putin, tried to implement a new design for the armed forces that involved increasing professional units backed up by a reserve force. To this end, a plan was proposed in April 2003. The political leadership intended to set up armed forces able to rival those of the West.

In October 2003, Sergey Ivanov presented to the High Command and Putin "Current Development Objectives for the Armed Forces of the Russian Federation." The "Ivanov doctrine" described the main paths to reorganization, in terms of budgetary and international constraints, and defined threats and possible missions for the armed forces. The document was supposed to mark the end of troubled times and was widely exploited in the media to illustrate Ivanov and Putin's abilities to reform the military, an institution largely regarded as unable to change. This document was presented as a sort of final point to a rapid and deep transformation process. However, it was the implementation, not the production, of this document that was the real challenge.[34]

Despite the media's tendency to present this document as a significant improvement in the relationship between the civil and military institutions, several analysts were quick to highlight the tensions it provoked between the leaders of the two spheres. Several also questioned the likelihood of military reform. Indeed, Anatoly Kvashnin more or less openly resisted Ivanov's efforts to reform the military after Ivanov became defense minister. Putin and Ivanov increasingly came to the conclusion that it was not only a personality issue but also an institutional issue, in that a large number of senior officers shared Kvashnin's views.[35] To balance civil-military power and reestablish the chain of command—and, not least, to demonstrate its authority—the political leadership had to fire Anatoly Kvashnin.

Sergey Ivanov openly criticized the General Staff in January 2004, arguing that it was not completing its main task of "situational analysis and development of troop deployment plans." In mid-2004, Sergey Ivanov assumed control of all aspects of military affairs, including operational matters. This clearly subordinated the General Staff to the Ministry of Defense and ended the rivalry between them regarding their relationship with the president. At the same time, Putin, through Ivanov, took advantage of a surprise attack by Chechen warriors in Ingushetia in 2004 to purge top officials from both the military and the security services, including, once again, Anatoly Kvashnin.

In retrospect, the Ivanov doctrine thus appears to have been a political tactic to recover the ministry's power over the General Staff. It can also be understood within the electoral context; legislative elections were to be held a few weeks later, in December 2003, and presidential elections in March 2004. Military reform thus constituted Putin's second campaign theme, the first being his offensive on the Yukos oil company. In the end, the heart of the Ivanov doctrine has been interpreted by most analysts as confirming the military's instrumental role in Russia's international discourse and action; as a new expression of ambivalence toward the West (still considered, among others, as a threat); and especially as an implicit renunciation of a thorough reform of the military.[36]

All analysts agree that the Ivanov doctrine clearly reflected Putin's evolution in managing state-military relations. However, they have put forward very different interpretations regarding the content and scope of Putin's change of course. Some believe that the document was intended to "calm the military,"[37] which was concerned about the possible consequences of reform. In reality, reform had already stalled, as two key questions had yet to be fully answered: What kind of country was to be constructed, and which threats should the military be prepared against?

Many facts, according to the specialist press, indicate that Sergey Ivanov ceased efforts at reform after July 2004. He would have benefited from a public campaign to demonstrate that his objectives had been met. According to the official presidential line, he had enough results to prove that reform had been achieved.[38] In light of these successes, Sergey Ivanov could have made military reform one of the key arguments in favor of advancing his own presidential credentials and gaining popular support.

Other analysts disagree with this reading of Sergey Ivanov's action. His statement that military reform had officially ended has also been subject to a more nuanced interpretation. The positive view was that the Ministry of Defense decreed the end of military reform to signify the end of the transition period. Indeed, various members of the security community had used this period as an excuse to defer organizational choices. Sergey Ivanov was likely inspired by the Polish and Hungarian examples of formally announcing the completion of reform. The more negative perspective was that other members of the security community would subsequently regard the efforts achieved to that point as sufficient and, therefore, they would not envisage any further structural changes. In fact, everything has gone on as if Sergey Ivanov were content, after Kvashnin's dismissal, with mere technical measures.

The General Staff remains a bastion that, given the personality of successive leaders and the situation in Chechnya, has had an increasing influence in doctrinal matters, strategy, and operations. The General Staff's institutional power is a legacy from the Soviet era,[39] and it has always benefited from significant autonomy, particularly in the Brezhnev years.[40] Within the Russian military, it acts as a gatekeeper of strategy, the ultimate shield for defending national interests. Boris Shaposhnikov, the most famous chief of the General Staff under Stalin, called it "the brain of the army." Shaposhnikov, marshal of the Soviet Union, largely contributed to the creation of the General Staff in 1935 and its subsequent reputation.[41] Under Yeltsin, General Pavel Grachev, the minister of defense, strove to limit the General Staff's autonomy by using the budget. Grachev, appointed at the age of 44, is one of the rare personalities capable of imposing his authority. His refusal to participate in the coup of August 1991, when he was commander of paratroops, won Boris Yeltsin's trust. He also was a hero of the war in Afghanistan and enjoyed great credibility among his peers, despite the General Staff's objection to his age and lack of strategic experience. From September 1993 onward, Grachev encountered the resistance of a group of officers led by General Mikhail Kolesnikov, head of the General Staff, and General Boris Gromov, the first deputy minister of defense. The minister of defense's position weakened after 1994, as he was unable to obtain budgetary approval by the Duma, and delays in payments increased. A series of scandals revealing the depth of corruption at the High Command weakened Grachev, who was nicknamed "Pacha Mercedes" for his fondness for powerful cars. He was then forced to join the war party led by Sergey Stepashin, head of the FSK (*Federalnaya Sluzhba Kontrrazvedki*, or

Federal Counterintelligence Service, predecessor of the FSB), and by Viktor Erin, the minister of internal affairs.[42]

The decision to go to war in Chechnya raised serious concerns and criticism within the security community. Seeking to avoid any head-on conflict with his minister, Mikhail Kolesnikov sought to limit his responsibility as much as possible; the armed forces' inconceivable lack of preparation is the best proof of the General Staff's extreme reluctance to send troops. In January 1995, the Ministry of Internal Affairs was given the role of supervising the federal forces operating in Chechnya. At the same time, Yeltsin was ready to detach the General Staff from the Ministry of Defense.

In reality, Kolesnikov's motive for removing the General Staff from the Ministry of Defense—transforming it into a "presidential institution" directly attached to the Kremlin, and confining the minister to the budget and military-industrial complex—reveals the continual instability of civil-military relations under Yeltsin.[43] Sensing the political risk of being too close to an autonomous General Staff with control over operations and management of troops, Yeltsin gave his support to Grachev once more, as Grachev established his authority over the generals. The first war in Chechnya was therefore also a war within the security community, one in which doctrinal and personal goals clashed in an overall atmosphere of considerably diminishing resources.

To reform the armed forces, the Russian president therefore had to construct a Ministry of Defense controlled by civilians from scratch. This could be accomplished by following the method deployed by Igor Gaidar, Yeltsin's prime minister, to destroy Gosplan (the Soviet State Planning Commission) in 1992, or, alternatively, by relying on a group of loyal generals—including Grachev in the higher ranks—to direct internal reform. Among the reasons, at least in part, for his choosing the second option was the fragile state of a society still traumatized by radical economic reforms (shock therapy); it could not weather another institutional shake-up. Destroying economic and military structures piece by piece would doubtlessly have multiplied the risk of overall instability. As well, Yeltsin was simply not interested in the armed forces, which did not contribute to his presidential power. Herein lies a highly significant difference between Yeltsin and Putin, who, having become president by interim appointment and not by elections, needed symbolism and the legitimacy of the state, largely fed by the security community.

At the outset of the second Chechnya war, Anatoly Kvashnin, and the General Staff assumed responsibility for the management of operations and at the same time limited the Ministry of Defense's role in nuclear weapons and program elaboration.[44] Kvashnin and his senior officers used the events in Kosovo and the seizure of Pristina airport to undermine Igor Sergeyev's authority, and to openly criticize his emphasis on nuclear weapons. The seizure of Pristina airport by Russian paratroopers was a clear violation of the chain of command within the ministry and more broadly within the government. It was a salient example of the political leadership's weakness. This operational supremacy clearly reflected an extension of the military's traditional zone of action, justifying an increase of its resources.

At the same time, the lack of political control over military objectives and the conduct of troops led to an impasse. There was virtually no established structure for detailing military and political objectives.[45] Therefore, the outbreak of the second war in Chechnya, beyond the personal rivalries, demonstrated the urgent need for structural reform. The initial phase of the war (winter 1999–spring 2000) corresponded with the culmination of the General Staff's influence. In August 1999, the Ministry of Defense was given responsibility for the military operations at the expense of the Ministry of Internal Affairs.

Given Kvashnin's antagonistic relationship with Sergeyev, Putin could have sanctioned him, but he would have then been faced with the dilemma of balancing the strong military leadership needed to impose operational decisions in the field with his own political future, which would have been dangerously affected by such a link to the military.

Four years later, Kvashnin's dismissal shifted the gravitational center of the presidential administration–General Staff–Ministry of Defense triangle to the benefit of the ministry. Most analysts regard this development as positive, as it is seen to reflect the desire to increase civilian control of the military. At the same time, this decision was an operational one: It was no longer acceptable to tolerate two parallel organizations such as the General Staff and the Ministry of Defense. For Sergey Ivanov, it was simply impossible to have two top officials reporting to the president separately. Compared to Igor Sergeyev, Sergey Ivanov benefited from his personal proximity to the president and, more importantly, from a stronger financial position. However, in retrospect, it seems that Kvashnin's dismissal was an end in itself; it did not necessarily signal the beginning of a reform process but rather the end of a cycle. The dismissal of Kvashnin was the pinnacle of Putin and Ivanov's victory over the military establishment.

Sergey Ivanov's action implicitly raised the issue of the elaboration and conduct of military strategy between the Ministry and the General Staff. Most analysts regard Kvashnin's dismissal as a positive development, though with varying explanations. Kvashnin, who was born in 1946 in Ufa, rose through the ranks of the military during the first part of his career in operational units. He joined the General Staff in 1992 before taking command of the military district of the North Caucasus from 1995 to 1997 and playing a key role in the conduct of operations in Chechnya. He returned to the General Staff as chief and then first deputy minister of defense, a position he held until 2004. In the meantime, he joined the Security Council and the Federal Antiterrorist Commission in 2000. He left the army in September 2004 to become Putin's representative in the Siberian Federal District. It is worth noting that Kvashnin constantly attempted to use the influence of the General Staff. He was strongly supported in those endeavors by Marshal M. A. Gareyev, one of the most respected and traditional figures in the Russian military.[46] Some believe it was this archaic and traditional military outlook that brought about his dismissal, while others believe that his qualities and loyalty were not enough to reassure Putin.

Kvashnin's successor, Yury Baluyevsky, is generally seen as an intellectual ready to compromise and most able to reorient the General Staff. Born in Ukraine in 1947, Baluyevsky is an officer of the General Staff and a 1980 graduate of Frunze Military Academy. He served in Belarus, in the GDR (1974–1979), and in the military district of Leningrad before joining the General Staff in 1982. After a stint in the Caucasus from 1993 to 1995, he returned to head operations of the General Staff before becoming chief of the General Staff in 1997 and deputy to Anatoly Kvashnin in July 2001. He succeeded Kvashnin in July 2004. Far more cautious than Kvashnin, Baluyevsky has never openly confronted his ministry. Only a month before Ivanov's appointment, he declared that "military reform is continuing."

Today, the presidential administration–General Staff–Ministry of Defense triangle should be working more smoothly, but it still lacks a cohesive direction. In short, changing the head of the General Staff resolved neither the structural imbalance nor the presidential grasp on the military. However, at this time, plans are under way to introduce a new joint structure between the General Staff and the military districts to better coordinate ground and naval force operations.[47]

Kvashnin's dismissal is seen as Putin's "main victory" with regard to civil-military relations, and it is probably Ivanov's as well. As far as Putin is concerned, it constitutes a peak in his political strength and desire for consolidation. For Ivanov, it corresponds with a political and personal wish to be involved in the top of the chain of command and to clearly subordinate the General Staff. The General Staff lost not only a particularly charismatic spokesman but also institutional influence.

Ultimately, this demonstrates the determination of Putin and Ivanov to lead a reform extending beyond the dismissal of the most emblematic figure of the military institution. It marks their joint will to rebalance the civil and military spheres to the benefit of civilian leadership with close ties to the security services. In their discourse, both men have managed to gradually disassociate the issue of state-military relations from that of military reform. In fact, state-military relations have never been dealt with head-on, as they affect the very nature and organization of the Russian elite. Sergey Ivanov's character, profile, and ambitions need to be taken into account when one considers how state-military relations developed during Putin's second term. By presenting reform as complete, Ivanov can focus on dealing with the Kremlin and public opinion.

Despite contradictory analyses of his action, Sergey Ivanov has undoubtedly consolidated his influence within the state since his appointment as defense minister. As is shown by his appointment as deputy prime minister in November 2005 and as first deputy prime minister in February 2007, he seems to have had enough room to maneuver to systematically bring in his own men, lead "mini-purges," and sideline the vestiges of the old military guard.[48] Indeed, expectations were high that he would succeed Putin.

However, in retrospect, Ivanov's achievements in the security field must be seen as less significant than Dmitry Medvedev's achievements in other areas. Medvedev's designation as Putin's official successor in December 2007 was significant with regard to the new balance in the Russian power structure. Despite not having a security background, Medvedev was pushed ahead of Ivanov because of his personal links with Putin and his influence on Russian business. If Sergey Ivanov's primary mission was to guarantee army loyalty to the Kremlin, then he was in large part successful. Three other key successes should be noted: the dismissal of Anatoly Kvashnin; the reestablishment of the Ministry of Defense as the top of the chain of command; and the succession by another civilian minister, Anatoly Serdyukov.

This sort of civilian succession is crucial in terms of civil-military relations. Anatoly Serdyukov was born in 1962 and educated in law and finance. He moved to Moscow from St. Petersburg in October 2000 to work in the Ministry of Taxes and was subsequently chosen to supervise the military budget. (He also happens to be the son-in-law of Vladimir Zubkov, whom

Putin appointed prime minister in September 2007.) Serdyukov is regarded as the first "real" civilian minister of defense because he has no background in the security services.[49] He was chosen because of his skills in management and finance, and he has been encouraged to promote civilian experts in the Ministry of Defense. As Putin's double term as president comes to an end, the question is whether this relatively new tradition of a civilian minister of defense will be continued in the coming years.

CHAPTER FOUR

"International Terrorism" as a Tool of Centralization

Putin's presidency has been marked by two central and closely related issues: the second war in Chechnya and the fight against "international terrorism." This theme, long a part of the Kremlin's national and international discourse, was magnified by 9/11 and systematically evoked during Putin's two terms as president. Whether political or military, the fight against "international terrorism" profoundly affects the security community: It has transformed the functioning of the Kremlin-military-security services triangle, as well as the relationship each has with society. By extension, it could be said that it directly relates to the Clausewitzian triptych of state-army-population, putting particular pressure on the population, which revels in "psychological denial"[1] with regard to the reform of the security community. In retrospect, the fight against "international terrorism" was Putin's main tool in centralizing power domestically. At the same time, it was one of the most consistent drivers of his security policy and foreign policy. As early as October 2000, he had presented "international terrorism" as "a global threat" and said that "Russia was one of the first states to encounter it."

Distrust of the Security Community

Surveys of public opinion provide an insight into the population's relations with the state and with the armed forces. Indeed, surveys carried out by the Public Opinion Foundation in July 2004 were revealing.[2]

- "Is military reform effective?": 40 percent of respondents replied positively, 31 percent replied negatively, and 29 percent voiced no opinion.

- "Are the armed forces capable of ensuring the country's security?":
  55 percent of respondents replied positively, 35 percent replied negatively, and 10 percent voiced no opinion.
- "Should students have the right to a deferral?": 83 percent of respondents replied positively, 10 percent replied negatively, and 7 percent
  voiced no opinion.
- "Do young men want to serve in the army?": 6 percent of respondents
  replied positively, 87 percent replied negatively, and 7 percent voiced no
  opinion.
- "What is the army?": 62 percent of respondents said it was life school-
  ing, 27 percent said it was a waste of time, and 11 percent voiced no
  opinion.

Other surveys indicate that the relatively low status of the armed forces in
Russian public opinion is still higher than that of the security services, and of
the FSB in particular. Low trust in the FSB can be explained by a high degree
of corruption within the organization, in stark contrast with the KGB, "which
was considered by the population as the least corrupt institution in Soviet
society."[3]

The armed forces inspire confidence through their ability to guarantee
security but suffer from a broadly negative image. This is mainly explained by
conscription, which is perceived to be a period of slavery (the *dedovshina*
phenomenon, or the violence that veterans inflict on new recruits with the
hierarchy's tacit consent), from which only the most socially privileged
escape.[4] Fear of conscription is manifest in the high rate of draft dodgers—
between 15,000 and 140,000 men. Corruption also accounts for the low regard
for the security services and their inability to fight terrorism or protect the
population. After the Beslan incident, for instance, 55 percent of Russians
polled did not believe the FSB was capable of fighting terrorism.[5]

Trust between the armed forces and the population is also required. Yet
harmonious civil-military relations are not limited to a good balance between
the leadership in the two spheres. Today this relationship is different from
Soviet times and could well provoke, in the years to come, high tensions in the
recruitment process. Indeed, according to demographic projections, the
armed forces will soon find it difficult to raise the contingents necessary to
maintain current personnel levels. This is complicated by the recent reduction
by law of the service period from 24 months to twelve.[6] Recruitment challenges are fundamentally changing how the forces operate. In response,
reforms are being undertaken within higher education establishments with

military chairs. To deal with the duration in military service, the General Staff has set up a system that is far stricter in granting conscription deferrals, and it has designed a new method of recruiting reserve officers through short contracts for study grants.[7]

Beyond numbers, several other circumstances threaten the traditions and habits of the armed forces. The limited availability of human resources, coupled with poor health and limited education of the enlisted contingents, undermine the very principles of the massive army. Russia, therefore, is on the brink of a historic break with tradition, in that, for the first time, it is no longer able to compensate for lack of military technology with sheer human numbers. The military High Command is, according to a journalist who specializes in the subject, customarily divided between "technicians" alarmed by the military's rapid deterioration and "magicians" who see Russian soldiers as having particular aptitudes enabling them to face all situations. The "magicians" have traditionally been the most influential.

The capacity for general mobilization today is a myth. According to several experts, the armed forces would be absolutely unable to mobilize, given their disorganization. The armed forces will be tempted to postpone structural reform once more and mobilize students while limiting deferrals, in an attempt to compensate for a reduction in overall numbers.

Yet such moves would be socially and politically explosive, as the mobilizations by students and their families in January 2005 have shown. It is important to remember that the issue of student conscription was one source of tension between Mikhail Gorbachev and his Ministry of Defense in 1989.[8] Like the Ministry of Defense, the Kremlin fears discontent among the youth and negative public opinion on their side. In pure political terms, the Putin–Ivanov duo's difficulty lies precisely in reconciling the High Command's need for conscripts and the nonmilitary aspirations of a younger generation.

In such a context, the military has no intention of placing students in combat units, according to a general, who regretfully took note of the deterioration in the quality of recruits. One expert has said he paid an officer $600 in 2000 to keep his student son from being conscripted. According to another expert, the debate over conscription deferrals is a smokescreen. When called up, students regard conscription as a waste of time, incompatible with the beginning of active life, and incapable of tackling head-on the main issues: abuse of conscripts by their superiors (*dedovshina*) and military slavery. They share a deep-seated fear of the military institution, with its roots firmly in the past, and at the same time strong pride in a country where the worship of force permeates all levels of society.

Beyond the inevitable discrepancy between civilian and military lifestyles, there is an increasingly worrisome social fracture between the military and the rest of the population, as well as within the security community. By way of example, the military was among the main victims of governmental projects on the "monetizing" of social benefits in early 2005. The suppression of privileges such as free transportation in return for a flat fee allocation resulted in an important drop in net earnings.[9] At the beginning of Putin's term, the real danger lay less in a *coup de force* than in the progressive marginalization of the armed forces.[10]

In 2005, a high-ranking officer and consultant summed up this social marginalization question the following way: "Why become a colonel, if it means earning $300 a month?" This issue of financial insecurity for both officers and soldiers has been crucial, and made more difficult with the strong symbolic devaluation of a military career compared to the Soviet era.[11] Both of these situations could be explained by operational inefficiency and lack of reform. What is more, the Russian military was no longer accustomed to a feeling of victory and pride, but instead knew only humiliation and impotence. Lack of career management—the refusal to allocate resources to the individual progress of personnel—was presented as one of the primary reasons for the failure of reform: Neither the Ministry of Defense nor the General Staff managed to draw up a system capable of identifying officers at any level of responsibility with the will and aptitude to undertake reform.[12] It is worth noting that interviews conducted in 2007 tend to indicate a better self-perception of the military and the security services. Undoubtedly, living conditions have improved, as Russia's economy as a whole has improved.

From society's point of view, the vast majority of analysts recognize the growing lack of interest of Russian society toward issues concerning defense and the state of the military. The weakness of civilian control is also explained by society's lack of involvement and civilian experts' poor capacity to influence. Such lack of interest in military matters reflects a more profound lack of interest for public action within a fragmented society, where everyone has worked toward individual survival strategies during the transition years. Moreover, because of the high degree of control exerted by the security services over journalists and experts in the field, it may also be the case that individual Russians are not fully aware of the present situation. Many analysts emphasize an urgent need to involve independent expertise on defense issues to prevent them from falling exclusively to military or service veterans. Such expertise would involve education on security issues independent of the armed forces and the security services, while simultaneously opening up the services to experts from outside its ranks. The current ratio of independent experts to those in the security community suffices to illustrate the sheer scale of such a project.

The relationship between and within the military and society are important vis-à-vis civil-military relations in two respects. First, the maintaining of conscription and the limited professionalization reflect a profound strategic disagreement on the nature and assessment of the military institution. According to experts, the debate is ongoing between those advocating a massive army prepared for large confrontation versus those advocating one more compact and capable of intervening in limited conflicts. However, in the official statements made by Putin and Ivanov, the second path was clearly the chosen one, even if it was not necessarily implemented correctly.

Second, conscription reflects the idea that the army has a pool of human capital that can be used in an almost discretionary manner. Exemplary punishments were handed out to officers accused of using their troops for private business. However, it is clear that conscription will continue to give the High Command very strong social influence within Russia and consistent leverage on the political leadership.

The pauperization of the Russian army was a key element in the evolution of politico-military balance during the 1990s. The social divide among soldiers, junior and senior officers,[13] and other layers of the population was also a key problem. The signs pointing to social marginalization or, conversely, to a nearing of the average living standards should be carefully noted, as they are valuable indicators of the state of civil-military relations. In this case, Putin's two terms as president correspond to improvements in living conditions for the military, even if deep inequities persist. At the same time, control over conscripts remains strong because of the corporatism of the armed forces, and absence of external influence.

Building an independent expert community would have been critical for both the evolution of state-military relations and the pursuit of reform. It was not at all supported by the Kremlin or the Ministry of Defense during Putin's tenure as president, undoubtedly because independent experts are mainly seen as proponents of Western civil-military models. Indeed, it is through these models that the main organizational outlines of democratic civil-military power distribution in Russia would be formed. However, the Kremlin strongly defended the principles of Russian "specificity." In addition, Russia's expert community has gradually become less interested in military issues, owing to lack of access to information, refusal to be manipulated, and, especially, lack of finances. The expert community has found it extremely difficult to find funding for research on this subject—aside from foreign funds, which always give rise to suspicion as to the work's ultimate objectives.

This control over information and expertise was particularly important for all issues concerning Chechnya. The two wars there are absolutely crucial to understanding the evolution of state-military relations under Putin. Both wars can be viewed as affecting Putin's personal power and explaining his behavior. To some extent, Putin needed the wars to strengthen his own position, to legitimize it, and to extend it beyond the military. The fact is that the conflict directly benefited part of the High Command, the security services, and the presidential administration, according to a journalist who has studied its financing. The Chechnya wars certainly caused divisions and highlighted the overlaps in spheres of competence within the security community, while creating a convergence of interests among the security community's various factions to impose yet again the primacy of security on society.

Operational Constraints and the Chain of Command

The main mission assigned to the security community by Putin after 9/11 was the fight against terrorism at the global level. This new role was difficult for the General Staff both in terms of organization and doctrine.[14] The combination of the concrete wars in Chechnya and the abstract war against "international terrorism" put the military under strain. While the wars in Chechnya were standard military operations, the fight against terrorism was an asymmetric conflict, since the terrorists had infiltrated and had to be routed out of the general population.

Domestically dealing with terrorism would involve a combination of judicial authority, police services, intelligence services, and, possibly, special forces. Fighting terrorism outside the national territory, however, creates challenges. Such was the case in February 2004, when two GRU officers and one diplomat were involved in a bombing in Qatar that killed the former Chechen separatist leader Zelimkhan Yandarbiev. The GRU operatives were arrested and sentenced to life in prison (Qatari authorities later permitted their extradition to Russia). Nevertheless, after the Beslan incident a few months later, Putin officially declared that terrorists "would be pursued, targeted, and killed abroad, and wherever they may be." The systematic neutralization of Chechen leaders (Emir Khattab in 2002, Aslan Maskhadov in 2005, and Shamil Basayev in 2006), were certainly inspired by Israeli tactics and experience in fighting terrorism. This task was assigned to the intelligence services and special forces. In purely military terms, by mobilizing 100,000 troops for the second Chechnya war (compared with 40,000 in the first one), the Russian armed forces adopted a tactic intended to suffer the fewest casualties possible, while killing as many Chechens as possible, including a large proportion of civilians. In other words, the armed forces—not being very comfortable with "the fight against terrorism"—saw an opportunity to reestablish the value of conventional capabilities. By ceding the fight against terrorism to other federal structures, the Russian armed forces would have potentially given up crucial leverage in terms of influencing decision makers. Yet the lack of a clear division of tasks between the armed forces and the security services—as well as the Ministry of Internal Affairs and its troops—engendered dysfunction in the chain of command during Putin's first term.

As in other fields, the presidential administration intended to play the leading role in the fight against terrorism. For this purpose, a unified command headquarters for special forces was established directly under the president. Putin alone—without any control by the parliament—could decide on the special forces' deployment abroad.[15] In February 2006, the National Antiterrorist Committee was created by presidential decree. It functions under FSB supervision. In parallel, Yury Baluyevsky reorganized military intelligence through a process of centralization and planning under his General Staff. This reorganization has contributed to modify the balance of civil-military relations in favor of the Kremlin.

Indeed, at the beginning of the second war in Chechnya, Putin gave his generals a free hand in conducting operations.[16] According to Pavel K. Baev, this war should be seen not only as key to a new type of leadership under Putin, but also as the only way the armed forces found to ensure their survival.[17] The General Staff's influence reached its pinnacle in 1999–2000, after which it declined for three reasons: the Chechnya quagmire; the reinforcement of Putin's power; and the consequences of 9/11 on threat analysis. During the initial stages of the conflict, the Kremlin was very good at securing consensus on the need for military intervention. Putin's initial trust in the "Chechen generals" progressively turned into distrust because of their tendency to ignore political leadership. That led Putin to reinforce the FSB's privileges, thereby depriving himself of numerous supporters among the officers (particularly in the intermediate ranks), who had not been a priori against reform attempts and the adaptation of the military tool to asymmetrical configurations.[18] Practically speaking, the most significant trait of this evolution was the FSB's growing involvement in both leading operations and attempting to achieve political stabilization. The end of military operations, announced in January 2001, was followed by the FSB's taking charge of the situation. In July 2003, troops from the Ministry of the Interior, including OMON units, were given responsibility for the military operations, which was significant in terms of the civil and military power distribution as well as in terms of the nature of the conflict.

Experience has demonstrated a lack of coordination on the ground among the various power structures involved, despite having set up a "united group of federal forces," or OGV (*Obedinyonnaya gruppirovka federalnykh voysk*). There were strong debates between the armed forces and the FSB about the means of the use of force. These debates reflected deeper divisions among the political leadership, the FSB, and the General Staff on the nature of the war itself.

The nature of these conflicts deeply divides the security community: Many continue to think in terms of large air-and-ground battles. This thinking is to the detriment of conflicts requiring a full range of options, from "high-intensity" and head-on confrontation of forces, to "low-intensity" conflict, crisis management, special forces operations, or security management, aided at times by units such as OMON.

Even within the institution, the state of the armed forces is understood differently. An influential group of generals continues to portray the armed forces as a combat-ready tool of great moral and operational quality. Others are instead alarmed by the inequality within the armed forces,[19] not to mention increasing social discrepancies.

By proposing a model mixing conscripts and professionals, Sergey Ivanov demonstrated that he had drawn lessons from his attempt at complete professionalization of a particular parachute division (Pskov), while at the same time avoiding directly affecting the military organization as such, because conscripts and professional soldiers continue to receive the same training.[20] By promoting the "mixed model," the Ministry of Defense sought to boost the idea of professionalization and the projection capabilities. The High Command regarded the model as a backhanded means of proposing more selective conscription, by attracting future professional soldiers while maintaining the principle of a large reserve that could be mobilized in the event of a major conflict.

Because it was linked by Putin to the global fight against "international terrorism," the second war in Chechnya had a direct impact on civil-military relations. With no objective other than crushing the rebellion, Russian authorities waged a war that mobilized a large part of the security community, damaged the country's international image, and threatened the very nature of the Russian Federation. The main victims were civilians, but fighters on both sides suffered heavy losses. Reports regarding the loss of federal troops vary widely.[21] In August 2006, the Ministry of Defense announced a death toll of 3,588 (a number lower than the 5,362 deaths the ministry announced in December 2004); the Committee of Soldiers' Mothers estimated losses at 14,000. Such a great disparity is explained in part by the fact that the ministry counts only those killed in combat, not those who die during evacuation or hospitalization. Moreover, each branch keeps its own statistics.

One thing is certain: Chechnya aside, the losses of the Russian army are comparable to those of an army involved in a low-intensity conflict. With Chechnya, the losses reached a politically significant level and hence they are highly classified. Indeed, losses in Chechnya can be compared to losses in Afghanistan during the 1980s. That being said, comparing the figures available with the losses of U.S. and British troops in Iraq shows that Chechnya is one of its most deadly theaters of the war against "international terrorism".[22]

The situation in Chechnya brought attention to the dysfunctional nature of the politico-military relationship. A civilian-military interface that generates more friction than harmony has affected the entire decision-making process at the highest levels. At the same time, the politico-military relationships are suffering from hyperconcentration at the presidential level. The dysfunction observed is threefold. First, the integrity of institutional and individual players has been severely questioned by operational conditions. Corruption has infected all levels of responsibility, so much so that the war has long been perceived by various experts as the security community's surest means to mobilize financial and human resources for its own benefit. Second, the functioning of the chain of command has suffered numerous fractures and constant overlaps involving the political center, different security organs, and regional commands.[23] Third, the manner in which the chain of command and forces are utilized on the ground has been the target of much criticism. Indeed, the "means of waging war" is ill-adapted to a conflict with an extremely volatile enemy and in which both parties engage in taking the population hostage.

By focusing on crushing the enemy and using "international terrorism" as a pretext to enlarge the conflict's political sphere, the Kremlin mobilized a force that did not correspond to a limited war or "counterinsurgency." Russian officers' strategic and tactical culture remained fundamentally imbued with experiences from the Second World War, with the High Command not having inculcated the principles of limited warfare. The High Command has preferred to hide behind the facade of efficiency in the media to avoid dealing with the dysfunctions in greater depth.[24]

However, the efficiency with which the special forces and intelligence services have eliminated Chechen leaders must also be noted. Openly entrusting the special forces and intelligence services with neutralization missions abroad explains why the political leadership was so keen to rely on that type of structure.[25] By way of example, in the presence of a Saudi dignitary in June 2006, Putin is claimed to have ordered his security services to find and kill those responsible for the murder of four Russian diplomats in Iraq. In July 2006, the Duma unanimously voted to allow the president to resort to deploying the armed forces and security services abroad for neutralizing terrorists. The decision to deploy was Putin's alone, eliminating the chances of confrontation, but exposing him personally in the event of a blunder.

Despite some undeniable successes, Putin gradually became locked in tactical logic that consisted of solving problems one by one. This power concentration had the adverse effect of diluting responsibility at lower hierarchical levels. In the event of a severe crisis, for example, the system became paralyzed, waiting for instructions from the top that were slow to come—and at times did not come at all. The "management" of the hostage-taking situation in Beslan was the most dramatic example of this organizational deficit.[26]

Confronted with an open-ended war, the security community has been involved in all its aspects. Nearly all the army's junior officers, for example, served at least once in Chechnya.[27] This situation has fostered a generational divide within the armed forces comparable to the one that arose in the last decade with the *afgantsy*, although in some ways it represents a return of influence with regard to the disillusioned Afghanistan war veterans. The two wars in Chechnya certainly have contributed to the cultural diffusion of violence within Russian society. In the beginning, Putin presented operations as a counterterrorist intervention intending to avoid Russia's "Yugoslavization." The Russian president saw Chechnya as a critical pivot in a region stretching between Morocco and the Philippines. The wars enabled Putin to put the parliament under his thumb in the name of federal unity and to exploit his popularity, media methods, and administrative resources to "eviscerate" the two liberal parties (SPS and Yabloko), marginalize the Communist Party, and mastermind the creation of the Rodina party.

The most remarkable result of this operation is the evaporation of Chechnya on the political agenda during Putin's second term, even while the armed forces and the civilian population continued to suffer losses.[28] Some analysts see Moscow as having gained the military advantage against the Chechen insurgents and are thus able to significantly reduce its troops' presence. However, this stability is fragile, as the Kremlin is losing control in the rest of the

North Caucasus (Ingushetia, Dagestan, Kabardino–Balkaria, and Karachay–Cherkessia).[29] Other analysts perceive that the second war in Chechnya is over and that the Kadyrov regime—by whatever means—has imposed order.[30]

The hostage taking in Beslan in September 2004 indisputably resulted in changes in three major areas: internal policy, state-military relations, and lastly, the general attitude toward security issues. The broad impact of the hostage taking deserves to be highlighted. Indeed, the event propelled Putin to the frontlines and enabled him to justify an administrative reorganization—one that was probably conceived before the crisis—intended to constrict public liberties.[31] The Kremlin's reaction to Beslan held instructive value for any prospective analysis. One expert has highlighted the radical political instrumentalization a "mega-Beslan" might engender in an electoral context: that of an emergency situation justifying exceptional measures and special powers.

The day after the assault, Putin explicitly disassociated Beslan from Chechnya by presenting the hostage taking as an attack of "international terrorism" and claiming that Russia would henceforth face a "total, cruel, war on a large scale." Analyzing this discourse reveals some confusion about Russia's post-Soviet geographical weakness, its nuclear status, and "certain people's" desire to break it up. In fact, Putin blended a classical understanding of interstate power relations and a transnational reading of mass terrorism.[32] Nine days after this declaration, he announced a string of measures intended to reinforce the country's unity and to combat terrorism, namely, the election of Kremlin-approved regional governors (thereby reinforcing the "vertical of power"); the proportional election of deputies from party lists (to suppress the last independent deputies and create stable parties); a plan to combat poverty in the North Caucasus (recognizing the region's unique situation); the creation of a new security system (representing yet another change to the distribution of responsibility among the various services); and the banishing of extremist organizations. These measures answered one of the Kremlin's imperatives: "International terrorism," to which Russia had been subjected, must be eradicated by all means—first and foremost being the reinforcement of the state.

In reality, "combating terror" was the defining aspect of Putin's presidency. He never considered Chechnya to be an ethnic conflict resulting from the collapse of the Soviet Union, but rather a conflict between civilization and barbarians who, he declared September 24, 1999, should be "shot in their outhouses." From the start, the Russian president made no distinction between terrorists and separatists. During his first term of office, the fight against "international terrorism" became formative both internally and externally.

At the start of his second term, the fight morphed into a global war against terror, a war presented as a struggle for survival in the face of threats to Russia's territorial integrity.

Putin's biggest challenge stemmed from the confusion of three distinct, if partly connected, issues. The first was the war against "international terrorism," which was the regime's watchword both domestically and internationally. The second was Chechnya, which, despite the losses and military means deployed, was presented as a counterterrorism operation. The third was the overall regional instability in the North Caucasus and beyond (Georgia). In this general framework, Chechnya remained a key component, as it continued to greatly affect the issue of political and military leadership.

This way, Chechnya has been the Gordian knot of Russia's civil-military relations. By integrating the conflict into the broader war against "international terrorism," the Kremlin attempted to downplay it. On the ground, the forces of the Ministry of Defense and those of the FSB had separate and distinct responsibilities, with the former controlling the Ministry of the Interior and railway's troops, and the latter controlling all the security services (except for the GRU) as well as border troops.[33]

Operations during the second war in Chechnya were better coordinated than during the first war. Dysfunctions reflected the sharing of responsibilities, resulting in bipolarization (General Staff versus FSB) and a fundamental confusion of what constituted domestic and foreign security. By turning the second Chechnya war into a theater in the broader fight against "international terrorism," the Kremlin exacerbated this confusion and struggled to clearly distinguish the roles of the armed forces, the intelligence services, and the police. It called upon these agencies because of their operational availability rather than their appropriateness for the mission at hand. At the same time, this confusion benefited the Kremlin, which was better situated to supervise the whole security community than during the first war.

Focusing the Defense Apparatus on Terrorism

Not all the assessments of Putin's actions with regard to civil-military relations are negative. The stability of presidential power, combined with the reinforcement of the authority of the Ministry of Defense against the General Staff, has created favorable conditions for pursuing long-lasting reform.[34] Unlike his predecessor, Putin managed to create conditions of stability at the expense of neutralizing every influential counterpower—albeit in the context of strong economic growth. Through his speeches, he is about to mobilize society through his focus on national unity. In terms of security, he deliberately chose to center this discourse on the terrorist threat, thereby managing to federalize all areas of the security community under his leadership.

Several analysts have criticized the idea that the terrorism discourse was an attempt to unite the security community. They emphasize the manipulation of public opinion and the different administrative structures that such manipulation allows. All segments of the security community have had an interest in participating in the fight against "international terrorism" for two main reasons: They benefit from the allocation of resources mobilized in its name and from the exceptional measures they could use to reinforce their own influence within society. A third reason has been put forward by analysts closest to the Kremlin: The fight against "international terrorism" offered an unexpected opportunity to accelerate the reform effort and adapt the structures of the armed forces.

In this sense, the fight against terrorism is mostly understood by analysts as a "slogan for the FSB as well as for the Ministry of Internal Affairs," according to a journalist for the official Russian news agency. For him, terrorism did not become the first strategic priority for all parts of the security community under Putin, because "the defense of territorial integrity remains the decisive strategic stake" for the armed forces. Abroad, the fight against "international terrorism" is far from being perceived as a doctrinal framework able to encourage and ease the reform of the armed forces. In other words, as long as the system of general mobilization is retained, preventing investment in compact, well-trained, and well-equipped troops, the armed forces will be hopelessly unable to deal with asymmetric situations. According to Western criteria, this reform should go hand in hand with redefining the missions assigned to the security services in counterterrorism, with stronger emphasis on a policing and judicial approach than on a strictly military one.

"International terrorism" was a Kremlin construction rendered credible by the U.S. post-9/11 strategy. From this point of view, the immediate support given by Putin to the Bush administration was the best way to justify his threat perception. According to a journalist who specializes in such issues, the ideological argument put forward by the Kremlin was to justify the situation in Chechnya. For Putin, it was essential that the threat be used to blunt the sword of Western criticism of his regime. In this respect, the fight against "international terrorism" closely aligned with the Kremlin's and security services' perception of threat, which was to be exploited for domestic and foreign political objectives in the media.[35] Not all areas of the security community agreed with this threat analysis. The General Staff, in particular, continued to regard the main threat as coming from the expansion of NATO, according to one general.[36] China was also perceived differently, with political authorities notably in favor of joint military maneuvers while military authorities were far more distrustful.[37]

An evolution beginning with Putin's second term must also be noted in terms of threat perception. Because of its resurgence, Russia has been able, under Putin, to reconsider its security dialogue with the United States. At the same time, Russia was genuinely afraid of the so-called color revolutions in Georgia, Ukraine, and Kyrgyzstan. More crucially, the United States' difficulties in Iraq, its attempts to deploy antimissile systems in Poland and the Czech Republic, the disagreement over Kosovo, and the Iranian nuclear program created a new strategic context that opened up new opportunities for the Kremlin. Old-fashioned threats to security were back and no longer constricted the strategic debate to the fight against terrorism.

This new strategic context is a crucial development for Russian civil-military relations, because no definitive reorganization of the security community can be possible without a lasting consensus on the threats the security community must be prepared to face. The evolution of civil-military relations therefore also involves a ranking of strategic priorities. With this in mind, it is important to note the progressive shift in threat perception during Putin's second term. This evolution is clear, for instance, when we compare his statement just after Beslan to hunt down terrorists "wherever they may be" with his speech at the Munich security conference in February 2007 in which he accused the United States of "almost uncontained use of force" in its counterterrorism campaign and of trying to establish a "unipolar" world. Russia's status as a postimperial, or neo-imperial, power weighs heavily on the reconstruction of its security community. It is thus fair to say that the real stake for civil-military relations lies in a clear threat analysis. According to a former high-ranking military officer who is now a consultant, the United States is still seen by the armed forces as Russia's main threat—a view accentuated since 9/11 and the United States' interventions in the Caucasus and Central Asia. This former officer believes that Putin should state clearly that the United States does not represent a real military threat to Russia in the future; only then can he truly begin to alter the civil-military balance. Given the degradation of the relationship between the United States and Russia since 2005, however, such a declaration is highly unlikely. Far from fostering a coherent clarification of threats, Putin has offered only ambiguous variations of the threats, which enabled the armed forces to cultivate fear and postpone any reorganization.

After eight years of Putin, the Russian elite is still deeply divided with regard to strategic representation: how to rank direct and indirect threats, or what type of alliance to pursue. Broadly speaking, three major schools of thought continue to collide.[38] The first consists of firm traditionalists for whom Russia's strategic situation is similar to that of the USSR: The United States and NATO still pose the main threat, while countries such as North Korea, Iran, and Cuba are seen as potential partners. The second school comprises pragmatists, for whom the major security challenges are conflicts of low intensity around the Russian Federation; the proliferation of weapons of mass destruction; and international terrorism. Faced with security issues similar to those in the West, Russia cannot avoid a complete overhaul of its armed forces. Moreover, this school supports the principle of a lasting rapprochement with the West in order to integrate Russia into the knowledge-based economy. The third school believes in the principle of a multipolar world in which there is no longer a unified West. From this perspective, it would be prudent for Russia to create informal coalitions—including with European capitals, China, India, and Iran—depending on the situation. This last school aims to maximize energy assets and avoid any direct confrontation with other major powers, while always attempting to weaken American unilateralism.

All three schools of thought have influenced Putin, although strands of thought from the latter two are most prominent in his policies. To a large extent, the pragmatic approach could best sum up his first term of office, while the multipolar approach dominated the second one. It is possible to draw parallels between the Yeltsin and Putin years with regard to relations with the West and to the instrumentalization of relations with countries such as China and Iran. While having different messages as well as means, both Yeltsin and Putin began with a declared desire to anchor Russia to the West and end Eurasian leanings.

From this perspective, the fight against terrorism is essential insofar as it is situated at the juncture of all these different schools of thought. Few contest the urgency of its relevance, even if, as a threat, it is understood differently by the various schools of thought. In a sense, the fight against terrorism provided Putin with the opportunity to unite the domestic-foreign interface and reinforce the importance of the security services in the entire politico-military system, since the fight against terrorism became, as Putin articulated in an address to the FSB command on January 15, 2004, the FSB's primary mission.

Yet the origin of the attacks in Moscow in 1999 continues to fuel suspicion about the security services.[39] This situation has resulted in a strategic fork on the road to Russia's societal development: to combat terrorism by tightening the grip on a society that, thanks to strong economic growth, is constantly opening up and changing, or to live with terrorism by relying on a society that would not support the constraints related to "unavoidable terrorism," precisely because of the freedom it enjoys. In other words, as an eminently strategic issue, terrorism, in theory, affects the Kremlin's political projects but in practice does not exist. Added to this, it directly affects the relation between the state and the society by feeding a consistent feeling of threat.

During Putin's two terms, despite having the fight against "international terrorism" on its agenda, the security community did not settle on common objectives. This situation results from excessive exploitation of the terrorist threat by the Kremlin and a declaration of war—with no precise aim or time frame—against a phenomenon that is in reality diffused. Yet the terrorist threat is seen differently by the various components of the security community. The restructuring of the security community, following a common strategic analysis—one that was supported, even encouraged, by the Kremlin—still does not appear to be complete. The old saying that "the Russian army is never as strong as it claims and never as weak as it seems" must not, however, be ignored. Indeed, the second war in Chechnya showed that the armed forces learned a number of operational lessons from their previous defeat. Moreover, Russian forces are carrying out exercises unequaled in scope since the fall of the USSR. Finally, the armed forces are benefiting from a new cycle in acquiring weapons systems, which will certainly significantly improve their operational capacity.

The crisscrossing evolutions of civil-military relations and military reform therefore cannot be disassociated from threat analysis, which is based mainly on "international terrorism." Declarations by civilian and military authorities, as well as meetings conducted in Moscow, reveal persistent confusion. This confusion was probably accentuated after the claim that military reform had been completed. Threat perception is a real challenge extending far beyond the military sphere, affecting the relationship between Russia and other countries, the construction of a postimperial national identity, and, hence, a mode of politico-economic development.

CHAPTER FIVE

Conclusion

This book has attempted to highlight the influential nature of the civil-military relationship on the Russian power structure. Indeed, the balance of the civil and military spheres was at the core of the Russian specificity promoted by Vladimir Putin. This book also has sought to analyze the identifiable trends in the evolution of civil-military relations under Putin, while bearing in mind the West's own model as a frame of reference. Such an approach is intended to gain a better understanding of Putin's Russia and of Russia in the near future.

Although the civil-military power distribution appears to be a technical subject, it is, in fact, a deeply political issue, irrespective of the regime. The balance of power is inevitably affected by any change that might occur in either of the two spheres. Through the civil-military relationship, the nature of a state's politico-strategic project can be assessed, that is, what is its understanding of the world; what resources does it have available; what is its willingness to modify its international environment. Studying the civil-military relationship also makes clear current modes of power, the sharing of responsibility in security matters, and, in certain cases, the will to act. Ultimately, it seems that the relationship can be viewed as an institutional contract, one that—contradictory though it may seem—is tacit between the civilian and military authorities. This sort of contract is never definitive but is dependent at all times on circumstances and times of war or peace. There are at least three provisions to it. Domestically, the first provision concerns the distribution of responsibilities. The "sociology" of power at the top enables conclusions to be drawn about the balances and imbalances, both institutional and informal, among the parties concerned. This approach should lead to an understanding of individual and institutional thinking, as well as the consequences of a fundamental distinction among the political leadership, the military, and the security services. It should also enable any potential transverse networks to be highlighted, where possible.

The second provision concerns the chain of command, that is, the decision-making process for resorting to force where domestic and external factors meet. The healthy functioning of the chain of command should be gauged by the designation of political objectives, the coordination of military targets, and the capacities of the mobilized units. The fluidity of the chain of command determines operational efficiency; in principle, it should also set forth the level of sufficient engagement and restraint in the use of force.

Externally, the third provision is what could be called the "power project" of the state; that is, its understanding of its external environment and of its determination to modify it. Consequently, this provision is intertwined with external threat analysis, on which the different parties of the security community do not necessarily agree, and with the formulation and implementation of a coordinated security policy. Not all states have power projects. Where these projects exist, they are difficult to ascertain, given that they entail a state's ultimate objectives. They combine as well a historical legacy, an understanding in an international backdrop, and some capabilities in power projection.

In Russia as elsewhere, understanding the relationship between the civil and military spheres is crucial to assess a country's power structure. In Russia more than elsewhere, this relationship is more crucial, given the state's historical heritage as well as its perpetual thirst for a sustained security policy on both the domestic and international fronts.

The Division of Responsibilities

Being unstable, the balance between the civil and military spheres in Russia has often been reduced to a sort of "militarization," inseparable from the rise in power of the *siloviki*. Yet this understanding is incomplete and even biased, insofar as it puts the military, members of the security services, and the presidential administration all in the same basket, implicitly supporting the idea that society is being brought into line as part of a neo-imperialist power project. It is, in fact, more appropriate to underline the rise in power of groups of leading capitalists who exploit key positions within the economic structure for personal means above all else. These groups—which combine *siloviki*, liberals, and *apparatchiks* from regional and federal administrations—are fierce rivals.

These internal battles are coupled with alarmist discourse on the risks faced by Russia and on its need to be respected on the international stage. And yet the current situation resembles a form of wheeling and dealing that is every bit as bad as the savage privatizations of the Yeltsin era. This depravity is far more real than any pursuit of a national project built on and embedded in sustainability.

Russia's imperial and Soviet heritage largely explains the nature of the fusion of the civilian and military elite. However, this fusion is not synonymous with "militarization" (in the sense of bringing society into line and central power being perfectly coherent), in that the *siloviki* are not a structured group. The *siloviki* are marked by intense rivalries and a high degree of heterogeneity, even without taking into account the deep divide between the armed forces and the security services. In this respect, the military is underrepresented within the top levels of the state (government, presidential administration, and Security Council) in relation to members of the security services. However, the armed forces are certainly not lacking in power; they even continue to exercise, and indeed reinforce, their power in four basic ways.

First, conscription gives the armed forces great influence over society. The political and social cost for future recruitment should clearly be kept in mind. Second, the armed forces guarantee Russia's strategic credibility by controlling the deployment of the nuclear arsenal. Third, the armed forces are connected to the military-industrial complex and, what is more, contribute toward the creation of military doctrine, that is, the definition of external threats and the necessary means to counter them. It is highly likely that the armed forces will continue to abide by their post-Soviet mission: of being the state's last rampart, loath to interfere as an institution in the game of political force and responsible for maintaining law and order. Fourth, given its heritage and the importance of the past in Russian politics, the military should continue to be a sacred cow in Russian society, but no longer the only one, as it was during Soviet times.

Regarding the distribution of powers, Putin's goal during his two terms was clearly to reestablish political authority over the military, something ignored during the Yeltsin years. Coming to office with a limited power base, Putin was careful in his actions. The second war in Chechnya gave him a chance to revive the military, while at the same time—and with the military's support—enlarging and legitimizing his own power. To reestablish authority on a very vocal General Staff, he appointed the first "civilian" minister of defense and was thereby successful in firing Anatoly Kvashnin. This victory was important for the development of civil-military relations because it clearly subordinated the General Staff to the Ministry of Defense.

The fact that Anatoly Serdyukov, who had no security background, succeeded Sergey Ivanov makes clear the Kremlin's wish to continue the "civilianization" of the Ministry of Defense. This process, however, is far from complete. As this analysis has shown, the idea that Putin was supported in this undertaking by the so-called *siloviki* is not easy to defend; more than any grandiose shared strategy, people with a security background were motivated by personal profits. In this way, the Yeltsin and Putin years are alike. By contrast, under Putin there was also a clear strengthening of the FSB as an institution, thanks to the March 2003 reform. Putin never, however, allowed the FSB to become so powerful that it could have undermined his own leadership. The securitization of many facets of life under Putin was obvious, but that does not imply that the FSB today has the same power as the Soviet-era KGB.

The Chain of Command

The chain of command is undoubtedly the cause of the greatest uncertainty for the future. The concentration of power around the presidency would have given Putin's administration much influence in strategic decision making—a capacity that would be gauged by the designation of political objectives and discussion with the General Staff of corresponding military objectives, as well as by the degree of tolerance toward the conduct of troops in the field. During Putin's two terms, it was difficult to judge the nature of the Kremlin's political objectives in Chechnya as part of a "normalization" process because Putin continued to equate separatism with terrorism. At the same time, it must be acknowledged that Russian forces had a series of military successes—even if some were merely symbolic, including the elimination of Chamil Basayev, who had taunted them for more than a decade.

One thing is certain: Chechnya has been at the heart of politico-military relations. In operational terms, the second Chechnya war was marked by improved coordination in the field and politico-military interfaces when compared with the first war. Military casualties, however, were higher than expected, not to mention the consequences for the local population. In this respect, the Kremlin and the security community, as well as the different parts of the security community fought to be held blameless for lack of success in Chechnya. The Kremlin demanded military results there. Yet having announced the end of military operations in January 2001 while continuing to suffer losses on a regular basis, the Kremlin had to continually justify waging a conflict that contributed directly to Putin's rise to power. Having politically survived the sinking of the *Kursk* in August 2000, Putin then used the sluggishness in Chechnya to gradually regain presidential control over the military's High Command.

To this end, Putin progressively turned Chechnya into a war against "international terrorism." This development takes into account the change in Chechen strategy to employ more radical measures, which from Dubrovka in October 2002 to Beslan in September 2004 had profound psychological effects on the Russian population. A particularly effective indirect strategy enabled Chechen terrorists to turn localized operations into acts of war, provoking purely military responses from the Kremlin. Moreover, Chechnya exposed how ill-adapted the Kremlin's counterterrorist mechanism was, at the cost of restricting public freedoms. The Kremlin now seems to be caught in a dialectic of terrorism and militarism that is currently impassable, insofar as "international terrorism" serves as a prism for threat analysis and saturates the public space. In retrospect, it appears that "international terrorism" was the main tool used by Putin to centralize his power in both the political and security fields.

This instrumentalization of terrorism soon proved to be burdensome. Tension arose with Washington partly due to the Bush administration's "promoting democracy" policies aimed at the post-Soviet region (at least until November 2005, when the U.S. military had to withdraw from Uzbekistan, where it had used an air base for operations in Afghanistan). The most radical elements of the Bush administration, which have taken a hard line toward Moscow, have always identified two issues on which to cooperate: the fight against the proliferation of weapons of mass destruction and the fight against "international terrorism." Indeed, "international terrorism" provided Russian diplomacy with a point of convergence not only with Washington and Beijing, but also with the authoritarian regimes of the CIS.

In Central Asia, Moscow exploited the following position: Unlike the United States, which found it ever more difficult to separate its discourse on the "promotion of democracy" from that of "international terrorism," Russia's discourse (especially after the May 2005 massacre at Andijan in Uzbekistan), dealt purely with security for regimes where the fight against "international terrorism" served as a pretext to intervene in all types of disputes. From this point of view, Moscow was offering security guarantees and political support for autocratic regimes while promoting its own security structures, such as the Collective Security Treaty Organization.

By connecting "international terrorism" and the proliferation of weapons of mass destruction, Moscow repositioned itself as the world's second nuclear power in an exclusive dialogue with the United States. This link, however, has gone beyond Moscow's constant effort to reconstitute the strategic credibility in which the Kremlin and the armed forces—with all parts in the mix—are vested. It must not be forgotten that the Russian authorities regard this risk as real. The West tends to forget that in 1996 Chamil Basayev managed to leave radioactive elements in a park in Moscow. A "mega-Beslan" scenario is often referred to within Russia's expert community.

The fight against "international terrorism" was also a useful partner for Russia's security policy of justifying preemptive action. General Baluyevsky has suggested the possibility of preemptive action in the Caucasus; his message, delivered on more than one occasion, seems to be addressed directly to Tbilisi. More recently, the FSB's scope for action was extended, after the assassination of four Russian diplomats in Iraq. This is Russian specificity at work: Putin publicly ordered his security services to eliminate the assassins. Unlike its Western counterparts, the Russian presidency does not hesitate to set explicit and unequivocal objectives for its security services. It is highly likely that in the future the Kremlin will accelerate its use of the services and special forces because they have been successful, at least from a strictly military point of view. It is uncertain as to how frequently the Kremlin will order such operations abroad.

Finally, "international terrorism" has extended the scope of the civil-military balance in the Kremlin's relations with society. In fact, "international terrorism" has determined, supported, and directed the Kremlin's discourse with the public on its security. The Kremlin preferred to talk more about "international terrorism" than about the situation in Chechnya, which gradually disappeared from the political agenda during Putin's second term.

Regarding the chain of command, it is important to bear in mind that the alignment of the respective units and commands during a crisis will influence the behavior of the Kremlin and the security community more so than doctrine. From this point of view, the chain of command was partly reestablished for the operations in the second Chechnya war. Management of the Dubrovka and Beslan hostage crises offered dramatic examples of operational failure in the civil-military power balance. Paradoxically, the experience of these crises did not affect Putin's leadership. On the contrary, they were the best way for him to strengthen his own power.

The Power Project

Russia's power project can be seen in the long term as trying to restore Russia's international *prestige*. The Russian power project is instinctively national and federal: Unlike other countries in Europe, Moscow does not envisage its future in terms of the integration or grouping of states. Maintaining the Russian Federation within its current boundaries is the primary objective of Moscow's security policy, which is why the state jealously defends its sovereignty. This guiding principle explains Putin's concern to find space to maneuver by loosening the vice grip of debt, refusing "junior partner" status with regard to Washington, and, more broadly, conceiving exchanges with his partners at a level of association, not integration.

Moscow's security policy is influenced by the vast expanse of Russian space. Moscow regards its territory as a crossroads of different influences within the heartland that forces it to conduct policy on several regional stages at once—a situation it cannot change, even if it wanted to. This situation explains the activism of a diplomacy carried out a global level (via international institutions and, in particular, its permanent seat on the United Nations Security Council); a regional level (via a network of regional organizations, such as the Shanghai Cooperation Organization); and a bilateral level (which puts it in a relation of force, especially in the post-Soviet area and vis-à-vis European countries). Consequently, under Putin, the sphere of action in foreign policy did not retract but expanded. He also showed willingness to regain influence exerted during the Soviet period (as in Algeria and Syria) and to form useful partnerships in the energy sector (with Venezuela and Iran).

Putin's policy was embedded in a strategic tradition that can be summarized as retaining freedom of action while doing nothing with it. Russia's relationship with other countries is still haunted by a foreign policy that is rooted in a national and postimperial identity. Although the policy is fundamentally changing, these relationships demonstrate the ambivalence of Russia's positions and its inability to form durable alliances. Moscow's failure at regional integration betrays the fact that Russia has found it impossible to commit to confidence-building measures with other states in the long term. This is due, in part, to distrust.

Distrust also is found at the heart of the Russian system and in the functioning of the civil-military relations that embody the country's power project. This project is fundamentally realist, consisting of weighing the balance of forces in all circumstances to seize the least opportunity for quick gains. To continue to hold its own, the elite has a real need for a threat system enabling it to justify a means of power organization; on a personal basis, as it is integrated more and more into the international elite, it holds fast, internally, to national and closed discourse. In this way, it is scarcely surprising to see an analogy between the Yeltsin era and the Putin era in Russia's relationship with the West and in the use of relations with China and Iran. With different tones and means, the two leaders began their terms claiming to be willing to join the West and ended their terms, following the historical reflexes of the politico-military elite, with leanings toward Eurasia.

To conclude, it is useful to emphasize an analytical error whereby it was believed that the civil-military balance in Russia could be reformed, as it was in Poland for instance, by following models imported from abroad. The security community's resistance to foreign influence provides an initial explanation for the strong reluctance to change, and this reluctance will likely continue in the next few years. Under Putin, the security elite has changed, but it has not yet turned away from reform to preserve a mode of organization. In addition, Western discourse on the need to reform civil-military relations is combined with an enlargement of NATO, which, paradoxically, would facilitate the immobilization of the Russian security elite. The prospect of NATO enlargement provided the High Command with an argument to extend analysis on the threat from the West and to conserve the principle of general mobilization, while pressure exerted on its southern flanks was used to justify its new operational needs. This state of tension and constantly deferred reform are indirect consequences of the willingness of some Western countries to integrate Georgia and Ukraine into NATO. Without opening the debate on the benefits and risks of NATO enlargement, it must be borne in mind that any enlargement would have repercussions for the balance of the civil and military spheres in Russia as long as Russia continues to defend the principles of specificity.

Ongoing analysis and interpretation of Russia's civil-military relations are needed to assess its power project more precisely. The difficulty for Russia's partners lies in understanding the difference in the momentum of change between the state and society. Profound and intense socioeconomic disruptions are coupled with resistance—and even regression—in other areas. This study is neither an invitation to be patient nor an exhortation for action; it aims to create the necessary distance to grasp the structural, but often forgotten, nature of the balance between civil and military institutions in Russia. As an elemental part of "Russian specificity," the relationship between these institutions will undoubtedly continue to affect the power distribution and the expansion of security policy, and, consequently, foreign policy. The more civil and military relations are taken into consideration, the better the understanding of Russia will be.

Notes

Chapter 1

1. Zoltan Barany, *Democratic Breakdown and the Decline of the Russian Military* (Princeton: Princeton University Press, 2007), p. 15.

2. For the first point, see: Christopher Locksley, "Concept, Algorithm, Indecision: Why Military Reform Has Failed in Russia Since 1992," *Journal of Slavic Military Studies*, vol. 14, no. 1 (March 2001), pp. 1–26. For the second point, see: Pavel K. Baev, "The Plight of the Russian Military: Shallow Identity and Self-Defeating Culture," *Armed Forces & Society*, vol. 29, no. 1 (Fall 2002), pp. 129–146.

3. Robert Legvold, ed., *Russian Foreign Policy in the 21st Century and the Shadow of the Past* (New York: Columbia University Press, 2007), p. 26.

4. David M. Glantz, *Colossus Reborn: The Red Army at War, 1941–1943* (Lawrence: University Press of Kansas, 2005), pp. 378–385.

5. Thomas M. Nichols, *The Sacred Cause: Civil-Military Conflict over Soviet National Security, 1917–1992* (Ithaca: Cornell University Press, 1993), pp. 1–14.

6. David Mendeloff, "Explaining Russian Military Quiescence: The 'Paradox of Disintegration' and the Myth of a Military Coup," *Communist and Post-Communist Studies*, vol. 27, no. 3 (September 1994), pp. 225–246; Brian D. Taylor, "Russia's Passive Army, Rethinking Military Coups," *Comparative Political Studies*, vol. 34, no. 8 (October 2001), pp. 924–952.

7. Brian D. Taylor, "Russian Civil-Military Relations After the October Uprising," *Survival*, vol. 36, no. 1 (Spring 1994), p. 6.

8. Eliot A. Cohen, *Supreme Command: Soldiers, Statesmen and Leadership in Wartime* (London: Free Press, 2002), p. 263.

9. Samuel P. Huntington, *The Soldier and the State: The Theory and Politics of Civil–Military Relations* (Cambridge: The Belknap Press of Harvard University Press, 1957).

10. John P. Moran, *From Garrison State to Nation-State: Political Power and the Russian Military Under Gorbachev and Yeltsin* (Westport: Praeger Publishers, 2002), p. 7.

11. Timothy J. Colton, *Commissars, Commanders, and Civilian Minority: The Structure of Soviet Military Politics* (Cambridge: Harvard University Press, 1979), p. 2.

12. Samuel P. Huntington, "Reforming Civil-Military Relations," in Larry Diamond and Marc Plattner, eds., *Civil-Military Relations and Democracy* (Baltimore: The Johns Hopkins University Press, 1996), p. 11.

13. Dale R. Herspring, *The Kremlin and the High Command: Presidential Impact on the Russian Military from Gorbachev to Putin* (Lawrence: University Press of Kansas, 2006), p. 119. In this book, the author deals with the following issue: "To what degree did the nature of presidential leadership affect the Russian High Command?"

14. Benjamin S. Lambeth, "Russia's Wounded Military," *Foreign Affairs*, vol. 74, no. 2 (March/April 1995), pp. 86–98.

15. Dale R. Herspring, "Deprofessionalising the Russian Armed Forces," in Andrew Cottey, Timothy Edmunds, and Anthony Forster, eds., *Democratic Control of the Military in Postcommunist Europe: Guarding the Guards* (New York: Palgrave, 2002), p. 197.

16. John P. LeDonne, *The Grand Strategy of the Russian Empire, 1650–1831* (Oxford: Oxford University Press, 2004).

17. Jean-Christophe Romer, *La pensée stratégique russe au XXe siècle* [Russia's strategic thinking in the 20th century] (Paris: ISC-Economica, 1997), p. 117.

18. Derek Leebaert and Timothy Dickinson, eds., *Soviet Strategy and New Military Thinking* (Cambridge: Cambridge University Press, 1992), p. 3.

19. Roman Kolkowicz, *The Soviet Military and the Communist Party* (Princeton: Princeton University Press, 1967).

20. William E. Odom, "The 'Militarization' of Soviet Society," *Problems of Communism*, vol. XXV (September-October 1976), pp. 34–51; William E. Odom, *The Collapse of the Soviet Military* (New Haven: Yale University Press, 1998).

21. Timothy J. Colton and Thane Gustafson, eds., *Soldiers and the Soviet State, Civil-Military Relations from Brezhnev to Gorbachev* (Princeton: Princeton University Press, 1990).

22. James H. Billington, *Russia in Search of Itself* (Washington: Woodrow Wilson Center Press, 2004).

23. Jacques Sapir, "Culture soviétique de la guerre" [Soviet war culture], in Thierry de Montbrial and Jean Klein, eds., *Dictionnaire de stratégie* (Paris: PUF, 2001), pp. 146–147.

24. Condoleezza Rice, "The Military Under Democracy," *Journal of Democracy*, vol. 3, no. 2 (April 1992), pp. 27–42.

25. Steven E. Miller and Dmitri V. Trenin, eds., *The Russian Military: Power and Policy* (Cambridge: The MIT Press, 2004), p. 217.

26. Dale R. Herspring, *Russian Civil-Military Relations* (Indianapolis: Indiana University Press, 1996).

27. Jeremy R. Azrael, *The Soviet Civilian Leadership and the Military High Command, 1976–1986* (Santa Monica: RAND, 1987), p. v.

28. Lester Grau, "The Soviet-Afghan War: A Superpower Mired in the Mountains," *Journal of Slavic Military Studies*, vol. 17, no. 1, 2004, p. 140.

29. Scott R. McMichael, *Stumbling Bear: Soviet Military Performance in Afghanistan* (London: Brassey's, 1991), pp. 38–39.

30. Robert M. Cassidy, *Russia in Afghanistan and Chechnya: Military Strategic Culture and the Paradoxes of Asymmetric Conflict* (Carlisle: Strategic Studies Institute, U.S. Army War College, 2003).

31. Patrick Cronin, "Perestroika and Soviet Military Personnel," in William C. Green and Theodore William Karasik, eds., *Gorbachev and His Generals: The Reform of Soviet Military Doctrine* (Boulder: Westview Press, 1990), pp. 137–140.

32. John Lepingwell, "Soviet Civil-Military Relations and the August Coup," *World Politics*, vol. 44, no. 4 (July 1992), p. 539.

33. Lilia Shevtsova, "Russia's Fragmented Armed Forces," in Diamond and Plattner, eds., *Civil-Military Relations and Democracy*, pp. 110–133.

34. Benjamin S. Lambeth, *The Warrior Who Would Rule Russia: A Profile of Aleksandr Lebed* (Santa Monica: RAND, 1996), p. 62.

35. Robert W. Duggleby, "The Disintegration of the Russian Armed Forces," *Journal of Slavic Military Studies*, vol. 11, no. 2 (June 1998), pp. 3–4.

36. Andrei A. Kokoshin, *Soviet Strategic Thought, 1917–91* (Cambridge: MIT Press, 1998).

37. Deputy minister for defense (1992–1997), he was appointed head of the Security Council (March 1998) but remained in the post for only five months. For an analysis of his career, see: Jacob Kipp, "Forecasting Future War: Andrei Kokoshin and the Military-Political Debate in Contemporary Russia," Foreign Military Studies Office (January 1999), <http://www.fas.org/nuke/guide/russia/agency/990100-kokoshin.htm>.

38. Alexei G. Arbatov, "Military Reform in Russia: Dilemmas, Obstacles, and Prospects," *International Security*, vol. 22, no. 4 (Spring 1998), pp. 83–134.

39. Andrei A. Kokoshin, *Strategicheskoe upravlenie: Teoriya, istoricheskiy opyt, sravnitelnyi analiz, zadachi dlya Rossii* [Strategic management: Theory, historic experience, comparative analysis, tasks for Russia] (Moscow: Rosspen, 2003).

40. Alexei G. Arbatov, "What Kind of Army Does Russia Need? The Contours of the Russian Military Reform," *Russia in Global Affairs*, vol. 2, no. 1 (January/March 2003), pp. 68–86.

41. Robert V. Barylski, *The Soldier in Russian Politics: Duty, Dictatorship, and Democracy under Gorbachev and Yeltsin* (New Brunswick: Transaction Publishers, 1998), p. 294.

42. David Betz, *Civil-Military Relations in Russia and Eastern Europe* (London: Routledge Curzon, 2004).

43. Barylski, *The Soldier in Russian Politics*, p. 291.

44. Alexander Golts, "Bremya militarisma" [The burden of militarism], *Otechestvennye zapiski*, vol. 26, no. 5, 2005, <http://www.strana-oz.ru/?numid=26&article=1150>.

45. Alexander Golts, *Armiya Rossii: 11 poteryannykh let* [Russia's army: eleven lost years] (Moscow: Zaharov, 2004).

46. Alexander Golts and Tonya L. Putnam, "State Militarism and Its Legacies: Why Military Reform Has Failed in Russia," *International Security*, vol. 29, no. 2 (Fall 2004), pp. 123–124.

47. Alexander Golts, "Glavnoe prepatstvie voennoy reformy—rossiyskiy militarism" [Russian militarism: the main obstacle to military reform], *Pro et Contra*, vol. 8, no. 3 (2004), p. 66, <www.carnegie.ru/en/pubs/procontra/Vol8n3-04.pdf>.

48. Edwin Bacon and Bettina Renz with Julian Cooper, *Securitising Russia: The Domestic Politics of Putin* (Manchester: Manchester University Press, 2006), pp. 8–9.

Chapter 2

1. Bobo Lo, *Vladimir Putin and the Evolution of Russian Foreign Policy* (London: Blackwell Publishing/RIIA, 2003), pp. 42–49.

2. The figures are from the following sources: International Institute for Strategic Studies, *The Military Balance 2005–2006* (London: IISS, 2005), pp. 158–168; International Institute for Strategic Studies, *The Military Balance 2006* (London: IISS, 2006), pp. 154–164; Brian D. Taylor, *Russia's Power Ministries: Coercion and Commerce* (Syracuse University: Institute for National Security and Counterterrorism, 2007).

3. Gordon Bennett, "Vladimir Putin and Russia's Special Services," Document no. C 108 (Swindon: CSRC, Russian Series), August 2002; Gordon Bennett, "FPS & FAPSI-RIP," Occasional Brief no. 96 (Swindon: CSRC, Russian Series), March 2003.

4. Taylor, *Russia's Power Ministries*, pp. 2–10.

5. Mark Kramer, "Civil-Military Relations in Russia and the Chechnya Conflict," PONARS Policy Memo no. 99 (Washington, D.C.: CSIS), December 1999.

6. Mark Kramer, "The Changing Context of Russian Federal Policy in the North Caucasus," PONARS Policy Memo no. 416 (Washington, D.C.: CSIS), December 2006.

7. Alexey Malashenko, "The Two Faces of Chechnya," Briefing, vol. 9, no. 3 (Moscow: Carnegie Moscow Center), July 2007.

8. Steven Rosefielde, *Russia in the 21st Century: The Prodigal Superpower* (Cambridge: Cambridge University Press, 2005).

9. The figures that follow come from Taylor, *Russia's Power Ministries*, pp. 10–12.

10. Barany, *Democratic Breakdown and the Decline of the Russian Military*, p. 57.

11. Yuri A. Ivanov, "Legal, Political and Budgetary Aspects of Civilian Control of the Military in Russia," *Journal of Communist Studies and Transition Politics*, vol. 17, no. 1 (2001), pp. 20–21.

12. Viktor Masnikov, "Deneg malo, potomu chto ih mnogo" [There is a lack of money because there is a lot of it], *Nezavisimaya gazeta*, September 22, 2004, <http://www.ng.ru/politics/2004-09-22/2_money.html>.

13. Walter Parchomenko, "The Russian Military in the Wake of the *Kursk* Tragedy," *The Journal of Slavic Military Studies*, vol. 14, no. 4 (December 2001), pp. 36–37.

14. Christopher C. Locksley, "A Russian Citizen in Uniform? Assessing the Applicability of the German Model of Civil-Military Relations to the Armed Forces of a Democratising Russian State," *Citizenship Studies*, vol. 4, no. 2 (July 2000), pp. 177–178.

15. Dale R. Herspring, "Vladimir Putin and Military Reform in Russia," *European Security*, vol. 14, no. 1 (March 2005), p. 140.

16. Dmitri V. Trenin, "Armiya i obschestvo" [The army and society], *Vedomosti*, February 25, 2004, <www.vedomosti.ru/newspaper/article.shtml?2004/02/25/72710>.

17. Lilia Shevtsova, *Putin's Russia* (Washington: Carnegie Endowment for International Peace, 2003).

18. Yury Pivovarov and Andrey Fursov, "Russkaya sistema i reformy" [The Russian system and reforms], *Pro et Contra*, vol. 4, no. 4 (Fall 1999), pp. 176–197, <www.carnegie.ru/ru/pubs/procontra/55826.htm>.

19. David J. Betz and Valeriy G. Volkov, "The False Dawn of Russian Military Reform," *Georgetown Journal of International Affairs*, vol. 4, no. 2 (Summer/Fall 2003), p. 49.

20. Bacon et al., *Securitising Russia*, p. 10.

21. Thomas Gomart, "Vladimir Poutine ou les avatars de la politique étrangère russe," [Vladimir Putin or the metamorphoses of Russian foreign policy], *Politique étrangère*, vol. 68, no. 3-4 (2003), pp. 795–798.

22. Thomas Gomart, "Politique étrangère russe: l'étrange inconstance" [Strange inconsistency in Russian foreign policy], *Politique étrangère*, vol. 71, no. 1 (Spring 2006), pp. 26–27.

23. Samuel Charap, "The Petersburg Experience: Putin's Political Career and Russian Foreign Policy," *Problems of Post-Communism*, vol. 51, no. 1 (January/February 2004), pp. 55–62.

24. Pavel K. Baev, "Putin's Court: How the Military Fits In," PONARS Policy Memo no. 153 (Washington, D.C.: CSIS), November 2000.

25. Herspring, *The Kremlin and the High Command*, p. 161.

26. Bacon et al., *Securitising Russia*, p. 77.

27. Dmitri V. Trenin, "Military Reform: Can It Get off the Ground Under Putin?" *Demokratizatsiya*, vol. 9, no. 2 (Spring 2001), p. 310.

28. Michael Ardovino, "Russian Soldiers in the Late Twentieth Century," *Comparative Strategy*, vol. 24, no. 1 (January-March 2005), pp. 64–65.

29. Vadim Soloviev and Igor Plugatarev, "Na armiyu mahnuli rukoy" [We mourned the army], *Nezavisimoe voennoe obozrenie*, April 29, 2005, <http://nvo.ng.ru/wars/2005-04-29/1_army.html>.

30. Herspring, *The Kremlin and the High Command*, p. 204.

31. Barany, *Democratic Breakdown and the Decline of the Russian Military*, p. 3.

32. Vladimir Ivanov and Igor Plugatarev, "Armiya ne doveryaet vlasti, a vlast—armii" [The army does not trust the authorities and vice versa], *Nezavisimoe voennoe obozrenie*, April 15, 2005, <http://nvo.ng.ru/concepts/2005-04-15/1_trust.html>.

33. Pavel K. Baev, "The Evolution of Putin's Regime: Inner Circles and Outer Walls," *Problems of Post-Communism*, vol. 51, no. 6 (November-December 2004), p. 5.

Chapter 3

1. Lilia Shevtsova, "Putin's Legacy: How the Russian Elite Is Coping with Russia's Challenges," Carnegie Moscow Center, Briefing no. 4 (June 2006), p. 2.

2. Olga Kryshtanovskaya and Stephen White, "Putin's Militocracy," *Post-Soviet Affairs*, vol. 19, no. 4 (October-December 2003), pp. 289–306.

3. Yury Andropov, the former KGB chief who led the USSR between November 1982 and February 1984.

4. For the retrospective aspect, see: J. Michael Waller, "Russia: Death and Resurrection of the KGB," *Demokratizatsiya*, vol. 12, no. 3 (Summer 2004), p. 351. For the prospective aspect, see: Barbara Vernon, "Les élites en uniforme" [The elite in uniform], *Pouvoirs*, no. 112 (January 2005), p. 76.

5. Taylor, *Russia's Power Ministries*, p. vii.

6. Thomas Gomart, "Russie: trop-plein d'énergies ou d'inerties?" [Russia: overflowing with energy or inertia?], in Thierry de Montbrial and Philippe Moreau-Defarges, *Ramses 2006* (Paris: Dunod, 2005), pp. 90–91.

7. Sergey Shapoval, interview with Olga Kryshtanovskaya, "V Rossii skolachivaetsya vlastnaya piramida sovetskogo tipa" [A Sovietesque pyramid of power is forming in Russia], *Nezavisimaya gazeta*, August 31, 2004, <www.ng.ru/ideas/2004-08-31/1_pyramid.html>.

8. Taylor, "Russia's Passive Army," p. 936.

9. For an analysis highlighting the direct involvement of the KGB in the strong periods of Soviet political history (a subject still highly debated by historians), see: Jeremy R. Azrael, *The KGB in Kremlin Politics* (Santa Monica: RAND, 1989).

10. Olga Kryshtanovskaya and Stephen White, "Inside the Putin Court: A Research Note," *Europe-Asia Studies*, vol. 57, no. 7 (November 2005), pp. 1065–1075.

11. Interview with the author.

12. Keir Giles, "Pay and Allowances in the Russian Armed Forces: A Guidance Note," Document no. 07/19 (Swindon: CSRC, Russian Series), June 2007.

13. Baev, "The Evolution of Putin's Regime," pp. 3–4.

14. Carolina Vendil Pallin, "The Russian Power Ministries: Tool and Insurance of Power,"

Journal of Slavic Military Studies, vol. 20, no. 1 (January 2007), pp. 1–25; Bettina Renz, "Putin's Militocracy? An Alternative Interpretation of Siloviki in Contemporary Russian Politics," *Europe-Asia Studies*, vol. 58, no. 6 (September 2006), pp. 903–924.

15. Pavel K. Baev, "Instrumentalizing Counterterrorism for Regime Consolidation in Putin's Russia," *Studies in Conflict and Terrorism*, vol. 27, no. 4 (July 2004), p. 341.

16. Vadim Soloviev and Vladimir Atlasov, "President rezko menyaet kurs voennogo reformirovaniya" [The president radically changes the course of military reform], *Nezavisimoe voennoe obozrenie*, August 4, 2000, <http://nvo.ng.ru/forces/2000-08-04/1_reforma.html>.

17. Andrey Korbut and Dmitry Nikolayev, "Kreml obedinyaet silovikov v regionah" [The Kremlin gathers the *siloviki* in the regions], *Nezavisimoe voennoe obozrenie*, May 19, 2000, <http://nvo.ng.ru/wars/2000-05-19/1_kremlin_unites.html>; Sergey Sokut, "Siloviki ukreplyayut svoi pozitsii" [The *siloviki* reinforce their positions], *Nezavisimoe voennoe obozrenie*, May 26, 2000, <http://nvo.ng.ru/wars/2000-05-26/1_siloviki.html>.

18. Herspring, *The Kremlin and the High Command*, p. 156.

19. Barany, *Democratic Breakdown and the Decline of the Russian Military*, p. 156.

20. Irina Isakova, "Russian Defense Reform: Current Trends" (Carlisle: Strategic Studies Institute, 2006), p. 56.

21. Guy Chazan, "Putin Orders Security Agency to Monitor Army's Allegiance," *Wall Street Journal Europe*, February 16, 2000; Igor Korotchenko, "Armeyskayay verhushka pod nadzorom FSB" [The army chiefs under FSB surveillance], *Nezavisimoe voennoe obozrenie*, November 28, 2001, <www.ng.ru/politics/2001-11-28/1_supervision.html>.

22. Baev, "Instrumentalizing Counterterrorism for Regime Consolidation," p. 342.

23. Mark Kramer, "Oversight of Russia's Intelligence and Security Agencies: The Need for and Prospects of Democratic Control," PONARS Policy Memo no. 281 (Washington, D.C.: CSIS), October 2002.

24. Daniel Treisman, "Putin's Silovarchs," *Orbis*, Winter 2007, pp. 145-146.

25. Gomart, "Russie: trop-plein d'énergies ou d'inerties?" [Russia: overflowing with energy or inertia?], pp. 90-91.

26. Sharon Werning Rivera and David Rivera, "The Russian Elite under Putin: Militocratic or Bourgeois?" *Post-Soviet Affairs*, vol. 22, no. 2 (April–June 2006), p. 141.

27. Brian D. Taylor, "Power Surge? Russia's Power Ministries from Yeltsin to Putin and Beyond," PONARS Policy Memo no. 414 (Washington, D.C.: CSIS), December 2006, p. 2.

28. Barany, *Democratic Breakdown and the Decline of the Russian Military*, p. 121.

29. Igor Korotchenko, "Generalnyi shtab zhdut peremeny" [The general staff is waiting for changes], *Nezavisimoe voennoe obozrenie*, June 15, 2001, <http://nvo.ng.ru/forces/2001-06-15/1_changes.html>.

30. Betz, *Civil-Military Relations in Russia and Eastern Europe*, p. 5.

31. Vadim Soloviev and Mihail Hodarenok, "President rokiruet *silovikov*" [The president inverts the *siloviki*], *Nezavisimoe voennoe obozrenie*, March 30, 2001, <http://nvo.ng.ru/forces/2001-03-30/1_president.html>.

32. Pavel K. Baev, "President Putin and His Generals: Bureaucratic Control and War-Fighting Culture," PONARS Policy Memo no. 205 (Washington, D.C.: CSIS), November 2001. For a development on this historic rivalry and also on the confusion readily encouraged vis-à-vis foreign countries, see: Amy Knight, *Spies Without Cloaks: The KGB's Successors* (Princeton: Princeton University Press, 1996), pp. 123-127.

33. Konstantin Simonov, ed., *Russia 2004: Report on Transformation* (Warsaw: Instytut Wschodni, 2005), p. 166.

34. Matthew Bouldin, "The Ivanov Doctrine and Military Reform: Reasserting Stability in Russia," *The Journal of Slavic Military Studies*, vol. 17, no. 4 (December 2004), pp. 619-641.

35. Herspring, "Vladimir Putin and Military Reform in Russia," pp. 149-151.

36. Marcel de Haas, "Putin's External and Internal Security Policy: Incorporating Analysis of the Defence White Paper of 2003 and the Terror Attacks of 'Nord-Ost' and 'Beslan,'" Document no. 05/05 (Camberley: CSRC, Russian Series), February 2005.

37. Viktor Litovkin, "La doctrine militaire russe" [Russian military doctrine], *Défense nationale*, vol. 60, no. 1 (January 2004), pp. 55-71.

38. Vadim Soloviev, "Minoborony vypolnilo raznaryadku po administrativnoy reforme" [The Ministry of Defense completed the standards for administrative reform], *Nezavisimoe voennoe obozrenie*, August 20, 2004, <http://nvo.ng.ru/forces/2004-08-20/1_reform.html>.

39. Condoleezza Rice, "The Party, the Military, and Decision Authority in the Soviet Union," *World Politics*, vol. 40, no. 1 (October 1987), pp. 55-81.

40. Brian Davenport, "Civil-Military Relations in the Post-Soviet State: 'Loose Coupling' Uncoupled?" *Armed Forces & Society*, vol. 21, no. 2 (Winter 1995), p. 177.

41. Glantz, *Colossus Reborn: The Red Army at War, 1941–1943*, pp. 387-391.

42. Matthew Evangelista, *The Chechen Wars: Will Russia Go the Way of the Soviet Union?* (Washington, D.C.: Brookings Institution Press, 2002).

43. Pavel K. Baev, *The Russian Army in a Time of Troubles* (London: Sage Publications, 1996), pp. 64-65.

44. Pavel K. Baev, "The Russian Army and Chechnya: Victory instead of Reform?" in Stephen J. Cimbala, ed., *The Russian Military into the Twenty-First Century* (London: Frank Cass, 2001), pp. 79-80.

45. Stephen J. Blank, "The General Crisis of the Russian Military," *The Journal of Slavic Military Studies*, vol. 16, no. 2 (June 2003), p. 10.

46. Steven J. Main, "Couch for the MoD or the CGS? The Russian Ministry of Defence and the General Staff 2001–2004," Document no. 04/09 (Camberley: CSRC, Russian Series), April 2004, p. 14.

47. Keir Giles, "Russian Regional Commands," Document no. 06/19 (Swindon: CSRC, Russian Series), April 2006.

48. Simonov, ed., *Russia 2004: Report on Transformation*, p. 170. See, for example, the sidelining of Leonid Ivashov a few months after he joined the Ministry of Defense: Igor Korotchenko, "Ministr oborony ukreplyaet svoyu komandu" [The Minister of Defense strengthens his team], *Nezavisimoe voennoe obozrenie*, July 19, 2001, <www.ng.ru/politics/2001-07-19/1_command.html>.

49. Vitaly Shlykov, "Odin v pole ne voin" [One soldier cannot win the war], *Rossiya v globalnoy politike*, no. 3, May-June 2007, <www.globalaffairs.ru/numbers/26/7704.html>.

Chapter 4

1. Baev, "The Russian Army and Chechnya: Victory instead of Reform?" p. 81.

2. Simonov, ed., *Russia 2004: Report on Transformation*, pp. 168–169; pp. 174–177.

3. Vladimir Shlapentokh, "Trust in Public Institutions in Russia: The Lowest in the World," *Communist and Post-Communist Studies*, vol. 39, no. 2 (June 2006), pp. 162-163.

4. Anna Politkovskaya, *Putin's Russia* (London: The Harvill Press, 2004), pp. 16-27.

5. Shlapentokh, "Trust in Public Institutions in Russia."

6. Alexander Golts, "The Russian Volunteer Military—A New Attempt?" *European Security*, vol. 12, nos. 3–4 (Autumn–Winter 2003), p. 62.

7. Alexei Arbatov, "Studenty, voennye kafedry i problemy rossiiskoy armii" [Students, military departments of institutes and problems of the Russian army], Briefing, vol. 7, no. 10 (Moscow: Carnegie Moscow Center), November 2005.

8. Bruce D. Porter, *Red Armies in Crisis* (Washington, D.C.: CSIS, 1991), pp. 39–40.

9. Igor Plugatarev, "Zaschitnikov otechestva zaschischat nekomu" [There is no one to defend the defenders of the homeland], *Nezavisimoe voennoe obozrenie*, February 25, 2005, <http://nvo.ng.ru/forces/2005-02-25/1_demarsh.html>.

10. Jennifer G. Mathers, "Outside Politics? Civil-Military Relations during a Period of Reform," in Anne C. Aldis and Roger N. McDermott, eds., *Russian Military Reform, 1992–2002* (London: Frank Cass, 2003), p. 36.

11. Igor Plugatarev, "Itog goda: lyudi v pogonah stali esche bednee" [The annual accounts: the military became poorer], *Nezavisimoe voennoe obozrenie*, December 24, 2004, <http://nvo.ng.ru/forces/2004-12-24/1_itogi.html>. See also: Igor Plugatarev, "Monetizatsiya lgot gromit armiyu" [The monetization of advantages is destroying the army], *Nezavisimoe voennoe obozrenie*, January 21, 2005, <http://nvo.ng.ru/forces/2005-01-21/1_shamanov.html>.

12. Christopher Donnelly, "Reshaping Russia's Armed Forces: Security Requirements and Institutional Responses," in Aldis and McDermott, eds., *Russian Military Reform, 1992–2002*, p. 311.

13. Igor Plugatarev, "Prikaz no. 345: trebuyutsya zagradotryady" [Order no. 345: barrage detachments are needed], *Nezavisimoe voennoe obozrenie*, January 28, 2005, <http://nvo.ng.ru/concepts/2005-01-28/4_leaving.html>.

14. Herspring, *The Kremlin and the High Command*, p. 186.

15. Isakova, "Russian Defense Reform: Current Trends," pp. 15–16.

16. Pavel K. Baev, "The Challenge of 'Small Wars' for the Russian Military," in Aldis and McDermott, eds., *Russian Military Reform, 1992–2002*, p. 195. Also refer to this chapter for a more precise description of the rivalries between different security organizations.

17. Baev, "The Russian Army and Chechnya: Victory instead of Reform?" pp. 75–76.

18. Baev, "The Challenge of 'Small Wars' for the Russian Military," p. 202.

19. Igor Plugatarev, "U Minoborony deneg hvataet tolko dlya 'blizhnego kruga'" [The ministry of defense lacks the funds for its "close entourage"], *Nezavisimoe voennoe obozrenie*, November 12, 2004, <http://nvo.ng.ru/wars/2004-11-12/1_dolgi.html>.

20. Alexander Golts, "Military Reform in Russia and the Global War Against Terrorism," *The Journal of Slavic Military Studies*, vol. 17, no. 1 (March 2004), pp. 34–35.

21. Fiona Hill, Anatol Lieven, and Thomas de Waal, "A Spreading Danger: Time for a New Policy Toward Chechnya," Policy Brief no. 35 (Moscow: Carnegie Moscow Center), March 2005.

22. Thomas Gomart, "Putin's Russia: Towards a New Combination of Military and Foreign Policies," *World Defense Systems*, vol. 7, no. 2 (Autumn 2004).

23. Dmitri V. Trenin and Alexey V. Malashenko with Anatol Lieven, *Russia's Restless Frontier: The Chechnya Factor in Post-Soviet Russia* (Washington, D.C.: Carnegie Endowment for International Peace, 2004), pp. 113–114.

24. Pavel K. Baev, "Putin's War in Chechnya: Who Steers the Course?" PONARS Policy Memo no. 345 (Washington, D.C.: CSIS), November 2004.

25. Henry Plater-Zyberk, "Russia's Special Forces," Document no. 05/50 (Swindon: CSRC, Russian Series), September 2005, p. 10.

26. John B. Dunlop, *The 2002 Dubrovka and 2004 Beslan Hostage Crises: A Critique of Russian Counter-Terrorism* (Stuttgart: Ibidem-Verlag, 2006).

27. Dale R. Herspring, "Putin and the Armed Forces," in Dale R. Herspring, ed., *Putin's Russia: Past Imperfect, Future Uncertain* (London: Rowman and Littlefield Publishers, 2003), p. 168.

28. Mark Kramer, "Guerrilla Warfare, Counterinsurgency and Terrorism in the North Caucasus: The Military Dimension of the Russian–Chechen Conflict," *Europe–Asia Studies*, vol. 57, no. 2 (March 2005), p. 258.

29. John B. Dunlop and Rajan Menon, "Chaos in the North Caucasus and Russia's Future," *Survival*, vol. 48, no. 2 (Summer 2006), pp. 97–114.

30. Malashenko, "The Two Faces of Chechnya."

31. Dov Lynch, "'The Enemy Is at the Gate': Russia after Beslan," *International Affairs* (London), vol. 81, no. 1 (January 2005), pp. 141–161.

32. Extract from a speech on September 4, 2004: "Today, we live in a time that follows the collapse of a vast and great state, a state that, unfortunately, proved unable to survive in a rapidly changing world. But despite all the difficulties, we were able to preserve the core of what was once the vast Soviet Union. . . . We showed ourselves to be weak. And the weak get beaten. Some would like to tear from us a 'juicy piece of pie.' Others help them. They help, reasoning that Russia still remains one of the world's major nuclear powers, and as such still represents a threat to them. And so they reason that this threat should be removed. Terrorism, of course, is just an instrument to achieve these aims."

33. Trenin et al., *Russia's Restless Frontier*, p. 136.

34. Bertil Nygren, "Introduction: Russian Military Reform in the post-September 11th World," in Yuri Fedorov and Bertil Nygren, eds., *Russian Military Reform and Russia's New Security Environment* (Stockholm: Swedish National Defence College, 2003), p. 9.

35. Vladislav Kramar and Igor Plugatarev, "Sergey Ivanov obyavil sekretnuyu voinu" [Sergey Ivanov declared a secret war], *Nezavisimaya gazeta*, September 10, 2004, <http://nvo.ng.ru/notes/2004-09-10/8_ivanov.html>.

36. See also: Vadim Soloviev and Vladimir Ivanov, "Genshtab vnov sporit s Minoborony" [The general staff is still in dispute with the ministry of defense], *Nezavisimoe voennoe obozrenie*, December 5, 2003, <http://nvo.ng.ru/concepts/2003-12-05/1_genshtab.html>.

37. Vladimir Ivanov and Igor Plugatarev, "Moskva i Pekin zakrepyat voenny soyuz na pole boya" [Moscow and Beijing to consolidate their military alliance on the battlefield], *Nezavisimoe voennoe obozrenie*, December 17, 2004, <http://nvo.ng.ru/wars/2004-12-17/1_china.html>.

38. Yury E. Fedorov, "'Boffins' and 'Buffoons': Different Strains of Thought in Russia's Strategic Thinking," Briefing Paper REP 06/01 (London: Chatham House, Russia and Eurasia Programme), March 2006.

39. Dmitri V. Trenin, "Russia and Anti-Terrorism," in Dov Lynch, ed., *What Russia Sees*, Chaillot Paper no. 74 (Paris: IES), January 2005, pp. 107–108.

Select Bibliography

This bibliography lists only works that have directly contributed to lateral issues. Articles from periodicals and the Russian press, which are given in the footnotes, are not listed.

Aldis, Anne C., and Roger N. McDermott., eds. *Russian Military Reform, 1992–2002.* London: Frank Cass, 2003.

Allison, Roy, Margot Light, and Stephen White. *Putin's Russia and the Enlarged Europe.* London: Blackwell/RIIA, 2006.

Azrael, Jeremy R. *The KGB in Kremlin Politics.* Santa Monica: RAND, 1989.

———. *The Soviet Civilian Leadership and the Military High Command, 1976–1986.* Santa Monica: RAND, 1987.

Bacon, Edwin, and Bettina Renz with Julian Cooper, *Securitising Russia: The Domestic Politics of Putin.* Manchester: Manchester University Press, 2006.

Baev, Pavel K. *The Russian Army in a Time of Troubles.* London: Sage Publications, 1996.

Barany, Zoltan. *Democratic Breakdown and the Decline of the Russian Military.* Princeton: Princeton University Press, 2007.

Barylski, Robert V. *The Soldier in Russian Politics: Duty, Dictatorship, and Democracy under Gorbachev and Yeltsin.* New Brunswick: Transaction Publishers, 1998.

Betz, David. *Civil-Military Relations in Russia and Eastern Europe.* London: RoutledgeCurzon, 2004.

Billington, James H. *Russia in Search of Itself.* Washington, D.C.: Woodrow Wilson Center Press, 2004.

Borovik, Artyom. *The Hidden War: A Russian Journalist's Account of the Soviet War in Afghanistan*. London: Faber, 1990.

Cimbala, Stephen J., ed. *The Russian Military Into the Twenty-First Century*. London: Frank Cass, 2001.

Cohen, Eliot A. *Supreme Command, Soldiers, Statesmen and Leadership in Wartime*. London: Free Press, 2002.

Colton, Timothy J. *Commissars, Commanders, and Civilian Authority: The Structure of Soviet Military Politics*. Cambridge: Harvard University Press, 1979.

Colton, Timothy J., and Thane Gustafson, eds. *Soldiers and the Soviet State, Civil-Military Relations from Brezhnev to Gorbachev*. Princeton: Princeton University Press, 1990.

Cottey, Andrew, Timothy Edmunds, and Anthony Forster, eds. *Democratic Control of the Military in Postcommunist Europe: Guarding the Guards*. New York: Palgrave, 2002.

Dauce, Françoise. *L'Etat, l'armée et le citoyen en Russie post-soviétique* [The state, the army, and the citizen in post-Soviet Russia]. Paris: L'Harmattan, 2001.

Desch, Michael C. *Civilian Control of the Military: The Changing Security Environment*. Baltimore: Johns Hopkins University Press, 1999.

Dunlop, John B. *The 2002 Dubrovka and 2004 Beslan Hostage Crises: A Critique of Russian Counter-Terrorism*. Stuttgart: Ibidem-Verlag, 2006.

Evangelista, Matthew. *The Chechen Wars: Will Russia Go the Way of the Soviet Union?* Washington, D.C.: Brookings Institution Press, 2002.

German, Tracey C. *Russia's Chechen War*. London: RoutledgeCurzon, 2003.

Glantz, David M. *Colossus Reborn: The Red Army at War, 1941–1943*. Lawrence: University Press of Kansas, 2005.

Golts, Alexander M. *Armiya rossii: 11 poteryannykh let* [Russia's army: eleven lost years]. Moscow: Zaharov, 2004.

Green, William C., and Theodore William Karasik, eds. *Gorbachev and His Generals: The Reform of Soviet Military Doctrine*. Boulder: Westview Press, 1990.

Hedenskog, Jakob, Vilhelm Konnander, Bertil Nygren, Ingmar Oldberg and Christer Pursiainen, eds. *Russia as a Great Power: Dimensions of Security Under Putin*. London: Routledge, 2005.

Herspring, Dale R. *The Kremlin and the High Command: Presidential Impact on the Russian Military from Gorbachev to Putin*. Lawrence: University Press of Kansas, 2006.

———. *Russian Civil-Military Relations*. Indianapolis: Indiana University Press, 1996.

Huntington, Samuel P. *The Soldier and the State: The Theory and Politics of Civil-Military Relations.* Cambridge: The Belknap Press of Harvard University Press, 1957.

International Institute for Strategic Studies. *The Military Balance 2004–2005.* London: IISS, 2004.

Kalika, Arnaud. *La Russie en guerre : Mythes et réalités tchétchènes* [Russia at war: myths and reality in Chechnya]. Paris: Ellipses, 2005.

Knight, Amy. *Spies without Cloaks: The KGB's Successors.* Princeton: Princeton University Press, 1996.

Kokoshin, Andrey A. *Soviet Strategic Thought, 1917–91.* Cambridge: MIT Press, 1998.

———. *Strategicheskoe upravlenie: Teoriya, istoricheskiy opyt, sravnitelnyi analiz, zadachi dlya Rossii* [Strategic management: Theory, historic experience, comparative analysis, tasks for Russia]. Moscow: Rosspèn, 2003.

Kolkowicz, Roman. *The Soviet Military and the Communist Party.* Princeton: Princeton University Press, 1967.

Lambeth, Benjamin S. *The Warrior Who Would Rule Russia: A Profile of Aleksandr Lebed.* Santa Monica: RAND, 1996.

LeDonne, John P. *The Grand Strategy of the Russian Empire, 1650–1831.* Oxford: Oxford University Press, 2004.

Leebaert, Derek, and Timothy Dickinson, eds. *Soviet Strategy and New Military Thinking.* Cambridge: Cambridge University Press, 1992.

Legvold, Robert, ed. *Russian Foreign Policy in the 21st Century & the Shadow of the Past.* New York: Columbia University Press, 2007.

Lieven, Anatol. *Chechnya: Tombstone of Russian Power.* New Haven: Yale University Press, 1999.

Lo, Bobo. *Vladimir Putin and the Evolution of Russian Foreign Policy.* London: Blackwell Publishing/RIIA, 2003.

Moran, John P. *From Garrison State to Nation-State: Political Power and the Russian Military Under Gorbachev and Yeltsin.* Westport: Praeger Publishers, 2002.

Merridale, Catherine. *Ivan's War: Life and Death in the Red Army, 1939–1945.* New York: Metropolitan Books, 2006.

Miller, Steven E., and Dmitri V. Trenin, eds. *The Russian Military: Power and Policy.* Cambridge: The MIT Press, 2004.

McMichael, Scott R. *Stumbling Bear: Soviet Military Performance in Afghanistan.* London: Brassey's, 1991.

Nichols, Thomas M. *The Sacred Cause: Civil-Military Conflict Over Soviet National Security, 1917–1992.* Ithaca: Cornell University Press, 1993.

Odom, William E. *The Collapse of the Soviet Military.* New Haven: Yale University Press, 1993.

Parrott, Bruce, ed. *State Building and Military Power in Russia and the New States of Eurasia.* New York: M. E. Sharpe, 1995.

Politkovskaya, Anna. *Putin's Russia.* London: The Harvill Press, 2004.

Porter, Bruce D. *Red Armies in Crisis.* Washington, D.C.: CSIS, 1991.

Pravda, Alex, ed. *Leading Russia: Putin in Perspective; Essays in Honour of Archie Brown.* Oxford: Oxford University Press, 2005.

Romer, Jean-Christophe. *La pensée stratégique russe au XXe siècle* [Russia's strategic thinking in the 20th century]. Paris: ISC-Economica, 1997.

Rosefielde, Steven. *Russia in the 21st Century: The Prodigal Superpower.* Cambridge: Cambridge University Press, 2005.

Rumer, Eugene. *Russian Foreign Policy Beyond Putin.* London: IISS, 2007.

Sakwa, Richard. *Putin: Russia's Choice.* London: Routledge, 2004.

Shevtsova, Lilia. *Putin's Russia.* Washington, D.C.: Carnegie Endowment for International Peace, 2003.

———. *Russia—Lost in Transition: The Yeltsin and Putin Legacies.* Washington, D.C.: Carnegie Endowment for International Peace, 2007.

Simonov, Konstantin, ed. *Russia 2004: Report on Transformation.* Warsaw: Instytut Wschodni, 2005.

Smith, Rupert. *The Utility of Force: The Art of War in the Modern World.* London: Penguin Books, 2005.

Staar, Richard F. *The New Military in Russia: Ten Myths That Shape the Image.* Annapolis: Naval Institute Press, 1996.

Taylor, Brian D. *Politics and the Russian Army: Civil-Military Relations, 1689–2000.* Cambridge: Cambridge University Press, 2003.

Trenin, Dmitri V., and Alexey V. Malashenko with Anatol Lieven. *Russia's Restless Frontier: The Chechnya Factor in Post-Soviet Russia.* Washington, D.C.: Carnegie Endowment for International Peace, 2004.

Index

About the Author

Thomas Gomart holds a Ph.D. in the History of International Relations from the University of Paris I (Panthéon-Sorbonne) and is currently the director of the Russia/NIS Center at IFRI (French Institute for International Relations based in Paris and Brussels). Since his appointment at IFRI in July 2004, he created a three-language electronic collection *Russie.Nei.Visions*@ifri, initiated several international projects, and published various reports.

Gomart's academic and professional background has been closely related to the post-Soviet space, and his expertise was enhanced by his international experience as a Lavoisier Fellow at the Moscow State Institute for International Relations (MGIMO, Moscow), Visiting Fellow at the Institute for Security Studies (European Union, Paris), and Marie Curie Fellow at the Department of War Studies (King's College, London). Thomas Gomart lectures on international affairs and on the geopolitics of resources at the Special Military School of Saint-Cyr Coëtquidan.

His publications include various articles in *Politique étrangère*, the *Washington Quarterly*, *Politique internationale*, and *Russia in Global Affairs*. He also contributed to several books on the Cold War published in France.

www.ingramcontent.com/pod-product-compliance
Lightning Source LLC
Chambersburg PA
CBHW011830020426
42334CB00027B/2997